WHITE STAR

PLACES AND HISTORY

greece

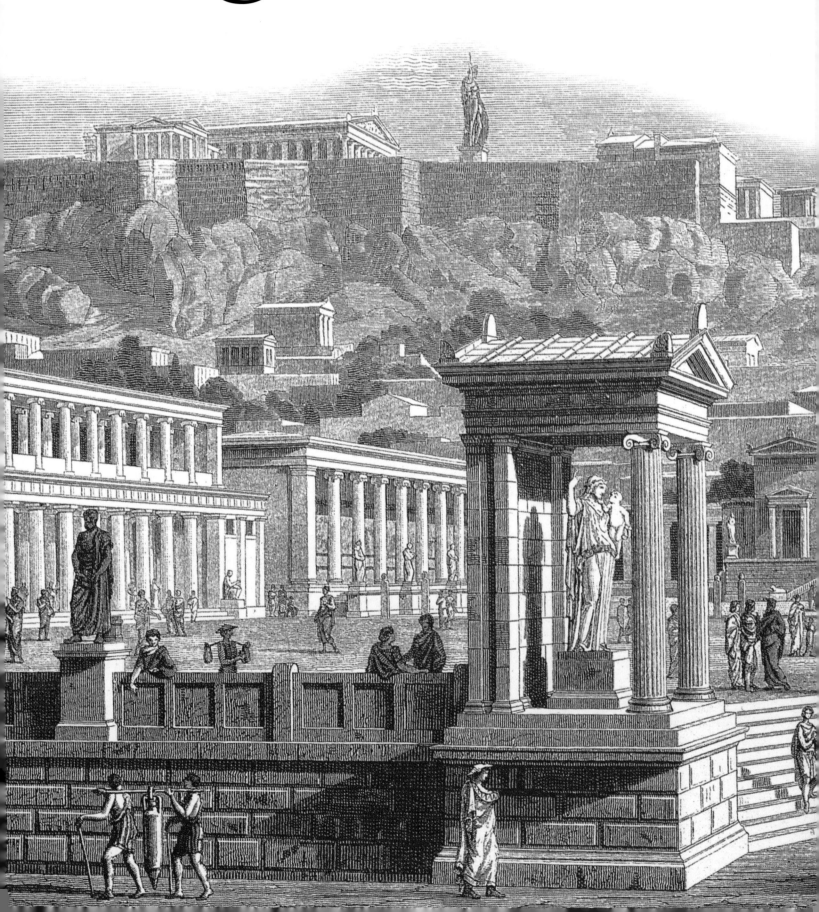

Text
Simonetta Lombardo

Graphic design
Anna Galliani

Translation
Ann Hylands
C.T.M., Milan

1 A bell tower on Santorini is silhouetted against the sea. The picture brings to mind the once popular "shadow puppet theater," in which the puppet Karahiosi personifies the archetypal Greek.

2/7 The agorà, Athens' marketplace, was the fulcrum of trade and political debate, at the heart of the city's most crowded and liveliest district.

3-6 A country of islands, Greece has countless ports: here we see the harbor at Antiparos, in the Cyclades.

CONTENTS

© 2006 White Star S.p.A.
New up-dated edition

© 1999 White Star S.p.A.
Via C. Sassone, 22/24
13100 Vercelli, Italy
www.whitestar.it

ISBN 88-544-0141-2

1 2 3 4 5 6 10 09 08 07 06

Printed in China

INTRODUCTION

9 top left Drama too, in the Greek world, was a collective rite of great religious significance. Spectators watched the punishment of those who had defied the gods, and man's own forms of justice.

9 top right The art and architecture of Greece are more than intuition. Classical temples are examples of strictly applied mathematical laws, and perfect relationships between real forms and optical perception.

I t has been said that no country - in Europe and the Western world at least - is better known than Greece, where for over two millennia the stunning sites of classical antiquity have been mirrored in a splendid sea. And yet, as well known as it is, Melina Mercouri, an internationally popular Greek actress and the country's Minister of Culture, used to say that foreigners identified modern Greeks with the men who built the Parthenon, invented drama and devised democracy. "You'd think, she wrote, "that Pericles died only yesterday and Aeschylus is still writing tragedies. What's more," she added with a note of bitterness, "if anyone knows about our struggle for independence from the Ottoman Empire it is only because Lord Byron took part in it." In fact the landscape, culture, and contemporary history of modern Greece is much more complex and multifaceted than most foreigners imagine it to be.

Undeniably, the sea is the most striking feature of the Greek peninsula and its archipelagoes. With a total land area of about 132,000 square kilometers, Greece has no fewer than 15,000 kilometers of coastline and no place inland is more than 100 kilometers from one of the two seas that wash its shores, the Aegean on the east and the Ionian on the west.

Historically, the Mediterranean has united the Greek people more than it has divided them. The philosopher Plato described the Greeks with their cities and colonies as "toads around a swamp." And although the sea has played a central role in the spread of ancient Greek civilization and in the country's importance as a trading nation, a role from which it still prospered in the early 20th century, Greece is essentially a land of mountains. They cover 80% of its territory, which is divided by three main mountain systems, the limestone Pindhos chain in the east, the eastern system that includes Mounts Olympus, Ossa and Pilion, and the massif of the Peloponnese, which is

8 The ancient art of Greece has always been religious in spirit: imposing civil monuments belong to the Roman vision of the world. These lions peering across the sea from Delos appear to be guarding the island sacred to the sun god, Apollo.

8-9 The Athens Acropolis is the best known and loved symbol of Greece. Of course, there is much more to Greek history than Phidias and Pericles but the symbolic value of the Parthenon even transcends its artistic splendor.

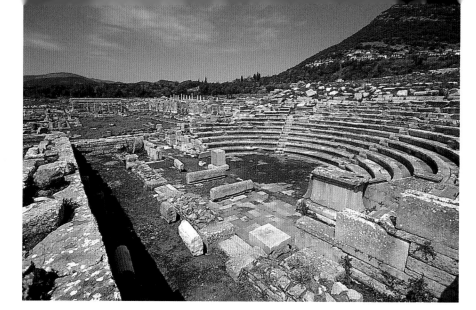

10 top The sun-baked cliffs of Poros are a fragment of Attica that emerges from the waters of the Saronic Gulf, far from chaotic, crowded Athens.

10 bottom Viewed from above, the delightful beach of Mirtos on Cephalonia looks like a crescent moon surfacing from the blue Ionian sea. Difficult access does not prevent visitors from going to one of the most popular places on the island.

the southernmost part of the Balkans. Many of the forests that covered Greece in Plato's day are now gone. Swathes of woodland were felled not only to accommodate post-war industrialization, but were razed over the course of millennia to make way for the pasture lands needed to rear sheep and goats. The mountain regions however, still provide a haven for many species of fauna. No fewer than 38 different kinds of falcon have been seen here during the migratory season. For resident species like the eagle and lammergeier vulture, the highlands of Epirus and Macedonia provide an ideal habitat. Large mammals like bears and the rare wild goats found in Crete, live in parks and nature preserves founded to ensure their protection.

Rainfall is scarce throughout the country, in the mountains as on the coast. It is only the omnipresent olive tree that can withstand the dry climate. All the same, wheat and sunflowers are cultivated extensively on the plains, and fruit orchards dot the hillsides. In smaller towns and villages, vegetable gardens and small, cultivated plots make a significant contribution to the meal table.

Even in Athens, the Greeks live a relaxed way of life that can add to the pleasure of each day's discoveries. Social life is conducted mainly out of doors, in spring and autumn as well as summer. Cafés are constantly crowded with people drinking *ouzo*, the national aperitif flavored with

10-11 An amazingly deep blue sea surrounds the island of Antiparos in the Cyclades, the sunniest archipelago of the Aegean. Sailing from island to island is a great way to experience the real spirit of Greece.

11 top The narrow entrance to the bay of Paleokastritsa in Corfu creates a lagoon effect. Nevertheless, the clear shining waters reveal the true nature of this sea.

anise, while nibbling at appetizing *mezas* or waiting for the grounds in their coffee to settle. (Remember, rather than make a tactless faux-pas, that although the coffee is served in a manner that elsewhere may be known as Turkish, here it is called Greek!) The Greek population is comprised of almost eleven million people. Ninety percent belong to the Orthodox church, the remainder include Catholic and Muslim minorities. The great majority of people live in towns and cities, many of which swelled to bursting in the aftermath of Greek-Turkish conflicts when waves of refugees from Asia Minor, towns around the Black Sea, Smyrne and Istanbul were forced into exile. More recently, wars and conflicts in the northern Balkan states, the splitting up of Yugoslavia, the civil war in Albania, as well as Kurdish oppression, have created large numbers of refugees who have sought asylum in Greece.

Today, the metropolitan area of Athens/Piraeus has between three and four million inhabitants, another million inhabitants live in Salonika. The rest of the population is distributed among coastal towns and villages, in most cases dependent for their livelihood on tourism, currently one of the most important sources of revenue for the Greek state. Greece also has the world's largest merchant fleet and a plethora of conventional industrial plants, including cement works and oil refineries.

The mountainous regions, which were primarily populated during the Byzantine and Ottoman periods when the coastline was under threat of attack by the Turkish fleet and not considered safe, have gradually emptied of people since the mid 1900's. Today it is not unusual, in Epirus, Macedonia and Thrace, to come across totally abandoned villages left to fall into ruin. Some 10 million Greeks have left not only their villages, but their homeland altogether, to live abroad, primarily in the US, Germany and Australia. The nation has benefited however, from so-called "emigrant workers' remittances," savings sent home by those who have found jobs abroad.

Ironically, a prominent feature of ancient Greek civilization was its ability to spread far afield along every Mediterranean shore from the Iberian Peninsula to the coasts of Asia Minor, not to mention settlements in Sicily and France. At the time however, like the British in India, the Greeks in the Mediterranean retained their own cultural identity, changing other peoples' ways to their advantage.

The ancient populations at risk of seeing ships packed with citizens of Athens, Megara or Thebes come sailing into their harbors, hardly welcomed these intrusive neighbors, for they were known to be hard bargaining merchants, determined settlers and on occasion, fearful pirates. The very origin of their name, "greek," promised no good (they have, after all, always called themselves *ellines*, Hellenes). The word "greek" contains the

14-15 and 15 top
The summer of 2004 finally restored to Athens the dignity of a host city for the Olympic Games. The picture below shows the thrilling closing ceremony, a monumental display of fireworks and music, applauded enthusiastically by the crowd. For the Olympics, the Greek capital hosted over 11,000 athletes, the highest number ever, and the Olympic flame traveled to all the continents for the very first time. Athens is one of the few cities in the world to have hosted the Olympic Games twice: the first time was in 1896, when the first modern Olympics were held.

16-17 Ancient and modern are combined in the villages of Skala, seen below, and Chora on the island of Astipalea. The defensive location of the second is justified by the succession of historical events that the village has lived through: the Ottoman invasion and piracy by north Africans and even local peoples.

17 top Three different periods exist together in Lindos on Rhodes. The Venetian citadel can be seen looking over the temple of Athena Lindia and the traditional village of island houses.

17 center As is the case on many Greek islands and coastlines, a Venetian castle stands guard above a village. This is Chora on the island of Kithira. The string of Venetian forts was especially efficient.

17 bottom Traditional architecture has remained in use on the islands as well as in inland villages. The photograph shows a small church facing the sea on Skiathos in the northern Sporades.

Latin root of *gregis*, and apparently referred to their reputation as sheep thieves.

When Greeks talk about the past, however, they are not talking about their Classical history, they are talking about events as recent as the war against Nazism and Fascism (recollections of which, among the elderly, are so very vivid) or of the colonels' dictatorship which only ended in 1974. Modern Greece is the outcome of complex historical events that most foreigners know very little about. Only in one respect do the Greeks live up to the image the rest of the world has of them: their passion for politics. At a time when democracies around the world are suffering from diminishing popular participation, politics is still the main topic of discussion and argument in the bars of Athens and streets of distant mountain villages. According to statistics, the Greeks are the most avid newspaper readers in mainland Europe and they have countless titles to choose from, including many local ones.

So beyond the familiar Grecian vistas of marble ruins and glittering seas, beyond the school-book stories of mythological gods and early philosophers, even beyond the ubiquitous pleasures of *ouzo* and olives, there is a varied landscape and a diverse people of rich identity, complex history and modern passions waiting to be explored.

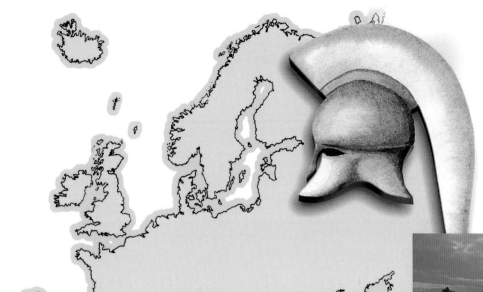

Pindos Mountains

Corfu, the Fortress

The isle of Skyros, Sporades

20-21 *The village of Monemvasia stands on a promontory to the south-east of Sparta. It is a natural stronghold that overlooks the coasts of the rich, powerful and fought over Morea, the modern Pelopponese.*

22-23 *All the spirit of the Mediterranean, with splendid cobalt blue water in a bay overlooked by a dry mountain, seems to be summarised in this picture of the sea on the island of Zakinthos.*

Crete, Istro beach

Sunion, Temple of Poseidon

Athens, Dyonisius teathre

Bulgaria

Turkey

Macedonia

Albania

Komotini

Xanthi

Kavala

Alexandhroupoli

Strimon

Salonika

Samothráce

Pella

Calcidian
Peninsula

Thassos

Kastoria

Aliákmon

Mt.
Athos

Konitsa

Pindos

Olympus

Kassandra

Sithonia

Lemnos

Igoumenitza

Meteora

Larissa

Thessaly

Skiathos

Aegean
Sea

Corfu

Ioannina

Parga

Kardhitsa

Northern
Sporades

Préveza

Acheloós

Lámia

Turkey

Skíros

Cephalonia

Agrinion

Lesbos

Chalcis

Chios

Euboea

Patras

Andros

Samos

Zante

Piniós

Peloponnese

Corinth

Athens

Olympia

Mycenae

Salamis

Keos

Youra

Tínos

Nikaria

Argos

Alfiós

Aíyina

Mikonos

Kalimnos

Náfplio

Sunion

Paros

Naxos

Kos

Ionian
Sea

Kalamata

Sparta

Evrótas

Mílos

Cyclades

Neapolis

Thira

Rhodes

Kithira

Dodecanese

Sea of Crete

Scarpanto

Crete

Canea

Iraklion

Knossos

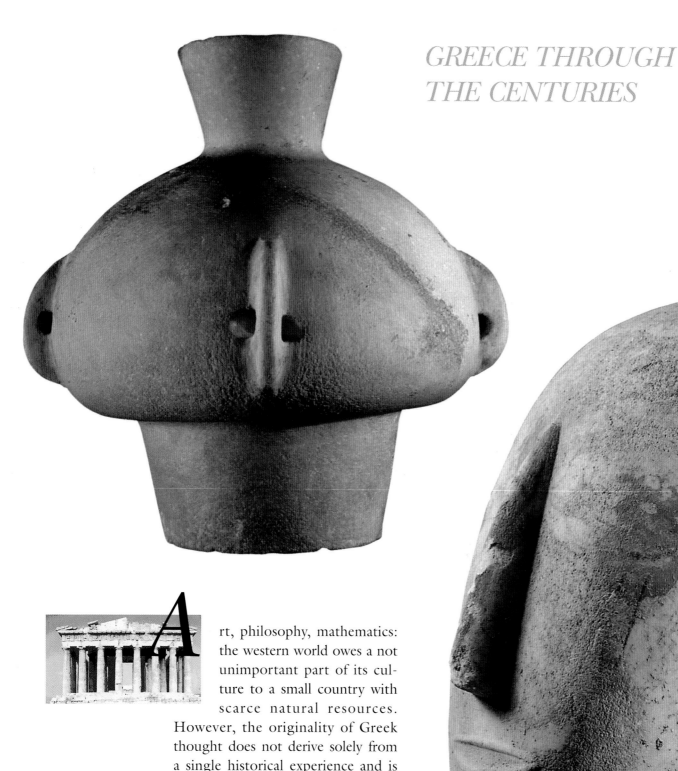

A
rt, philosophy, mathematics:
the western world owes a not
unimportant part of its culture to a small country with
scarce natural resources.
However, the originality of Greek
thought does not derive solely from
a single historical experience and is
not due only to the Golden Age of
classical Athens. The Greeks and
their culture have emerged from a
singular melting-pot, a pack of constantly reshuffled cards. This region
and its earliest neolithic inhabitants -
farmers and herders - were first over-
run by invaders from the steppes of
Asia Minor between 2600 and 2000
BC. The newcomers brought with
them craft skills like metalworking
and pottery, plus another total inno-
vation for this part of the world: urban settlements.

In 2000 BC invaders entered Greece
from the north: they were Ionians,

*24 top left Testifying
to the ancient culture
of Pelos (3200-2800
BC) are the striking
forms of this original
marble urn.*

*24 bottom right This
piece of a Paros idol,
found on Amorgos,
would not be out of
place in a
contemporary art
collection. Its
expressiveness is
derived from its
physical features: the
long straight nose, the
lips parted to utter
some ancient word.*

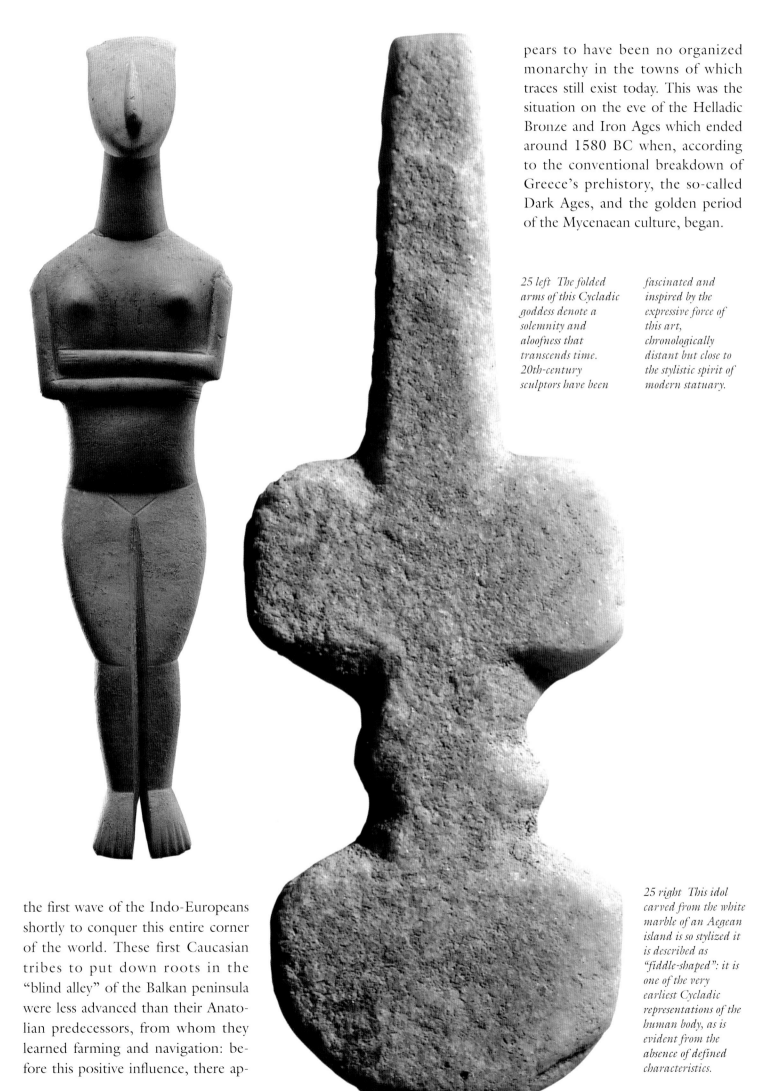

pears to have been no organized monarchy in the towns of which traces still exist today. This was the situation on the eve of the Helladic Bronze and Iron Ages which ended around 1580 BC when, according to the conventional breakdown of Greece's prehistory, the so-called Dark Ages, and the golden period of the Mycenaean culture, began.

25 left The folded arms of this Cycladic goddess denote a solemnity and aloofness that transcends time. 20th-century sculptors have been fascinated and inspired by the expressive force of this art, chronologically distant but close to the stylistic spirit of modern statuary.

the first wave of the Indo-Europeans shortly to conquer this entire corner of the world. These first Caucasian tribes to put down roots in the "blind alley" of the Balkan peninsula were less advanced than their Anatolian predecessors, from whom they learned farming and navigation: before this positive influence, there ap-

25 right This idol carved from the white marble of an Aegean island is so stylized it is described as "fiddle-shaped": it is one of the very earliest Cycladic representations of the human body, as is evident from the absence of defined characteristics.

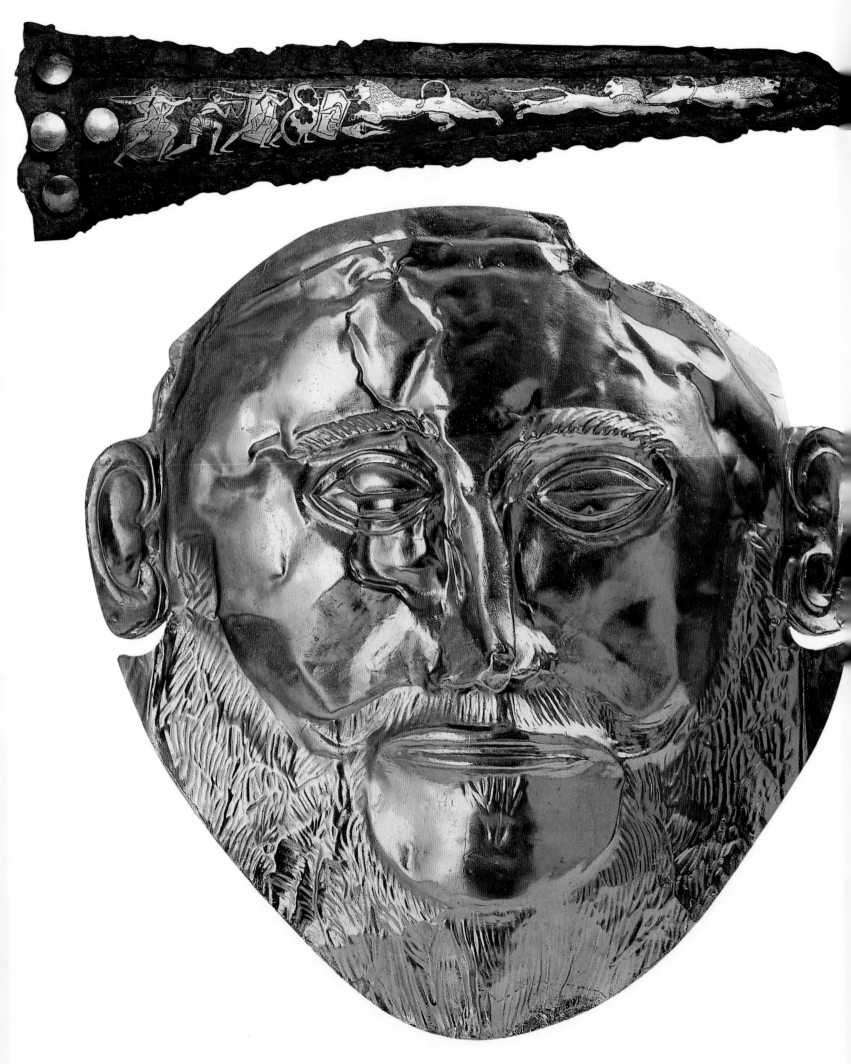

The second wave of Indo-European invasions had brought the Achaeans to the peninsula, at a time when the region was already feeling the effects of the growing expansionism of Crete and its lifestyle. The orientalizing culture of the Mycenaean age stemmed from a mix of the Achaean and Minoan cultures. Its most significant achievements were the palace-settlements (Mycenae itself, Athens, royal palaces modelled on Cnossus) and a centralized power structure based on a clearly defined pyramid of social classes and castes: beneath the king and aristocracy came officials and scribes and, beneath them, artisans and peasants. Slaves, generally enemies or foreigners carried off from their homelands, were a class apart. As in Asia government was exercised mainly in the form of city-states and rivalry between cities was frequent, as related in the *Iliad*. For Homer's poem is first and foremost the story of a truce among the

Achean cities, once such great allies that they joined forces to fight an excessively powerful neighbor (for in the broadest sense Troy too was "Greek").

This city of Asia Minor was not the only one to pay the price of the Greeks' expansionist ambitions: Crete, the other pole of the Mycenaean "revolution," also fell to the Achaeans in the 15th century BC. Not satisfied with the conquest of Crete, they soon established an intricate network of trade, political and cultural relations throughout the Eastern and Central Mediterranean.

The Achaean pantheon, partially derived from Minoan religion, penetrated various cultures, with its deities assuming different characteristics. Zeus was thus a "northern" god of lightening who wedded Hera, a short-tempered version of the mother goddess of neolithic origin welcomed into the religion of Crete. Also from this source came other deities: Athena, Artemis, Hermes, Poseidon, Hephaestus.

These gods also survived the last great crisis of prehistoric Greece, the invasion of the Dorians, Act Three of the Indo-European invasion (1200 BC). Like the earlier waves of migrants, the Dorians brought with them a less refined and structured civilization and a more male-dominated and bellicose religion than that of the existing local cults. Their arrival led to the destruction of powerful - and beautiful - Achaean cities but conquerors and vanquished eventually learned to live together, and to amalgamate. Dorian culture continued to prevail in Sparta, renowned for its closed, belligerent society.

It is the coexistence of different histories and cultures and their rivalry that created the melting-pot that was subsequently to produce the *poleis*, drama, painted vases, the alphabet, the great classical art that culminated in the temples. Historians regard 750 BC as marking the end of the so-called Early Archaic Period. Around that same time the ethnic concoction of peoples who then inhabited the Balkan peninsula acquired a common name, by which they are still known today: Hellenes.

28 top left This stylized bronze horseman exemplifies the Orient's influence on Greek art. Cavalry in fact never had a great tradition in Greek armies on account of the country's difficult terrain.

28 bottom right This bronze helmet in Corinthian style dates to around 500 BC. Found in the Archaic necropolis of Aghia Paraskevi, it belongs to the most glorious period of Greek civilization.

plains of Thessaly, was scarce. As always in such circumstances, the least fortunate were the first to leave, off in search of fortune or simply escaping from a hand-to-mouth existence. But like the poor Europeans who sailed to America 2,500 years later, the colonists eventually enjoyed the richest pickings. Between 700 and 500 BC the Mediterranean saw a continuous blossoming of Greek settlements: Naples, Marseilles, Constantinople... The colonists maintained close links with the homeland and the centers they founded soon became outposts of Greek culture and art. The Greeks as traders ventured to the furthest corners of the known world to find buyers for their fine-quality merchandise. Visitors to Dublin's archaeological museum, therefore, will see not only Viking ships but also splendid painted vases depicting mythological figures, and cups decorated with heroic scenes, finds unearthened on Irish soil.

In the 6th century BC the region's economy experienced a real boom: coinage was introduced, trade thrived and arts and crafts were truly established. As a consequence of these developments, law-makers set to work, determined to fix regulations for trade even before rules to govern civic life. In Athens, the most open and lively of the Greek *poleis*, Solon's and Cleisthenes's democracies were installed. It was the people's government that made political decisions, but of course "people" did not include everyone: certainly not slaves, or women, or the impoverished underclass.

Meanwhile Greece was growing, even beyond the territorial confines of the Balkan peninsula. The wealth produced by trade made the poor soil and hard life of its rural communities even harder to bear: grape vines and olive groves were abundant but corn, cultivated only in the fertile but arid

29 top left Heavy infantry, comprised of hoplites, provided the "crack units" of Greek city-states. They were armed with swords and spears, and well protected by bronze armor and a large shield.

29 bottom right Solon, one of Athens' most influential statesmen, introduced important reforms: for instance, he established that no citizen could be enslaved because of debts. His 590 BC constitution classified Athenians according to census and assigned them precise rights and duties.

Greece's classical period – as it later became known – stemmed, indirectly, from the Persian wars. Early in the 5th century BC the Persians gained control of the Greek colonies in Asia Minor, and then set their sights on the motherland.

The warring parties were seemingly ill-matched but the eventual outcome was an extraordinary surprise: in 490, at Marathon, the Athenians defeated the troops of the Persian emperor, Darius. But this was only the beginning. Ten years later, Xerxes, son of Darius, sought revenge. He attacked from the north, at the head of a huge army (Herodotus - admittedly a partial historian - spoke of 1,700,000 Persians).

At Thermopylae, a heroic band of 300 Greeks under Leonidas managed to block Xerxes and his men.

Meanwhile, off the island of Salamis, the Athenians and their allies led by Themistocles battled with the Persian fleet and won the day.

In 479 BC, the Persian land army was routed by the finally united Greek city-states.

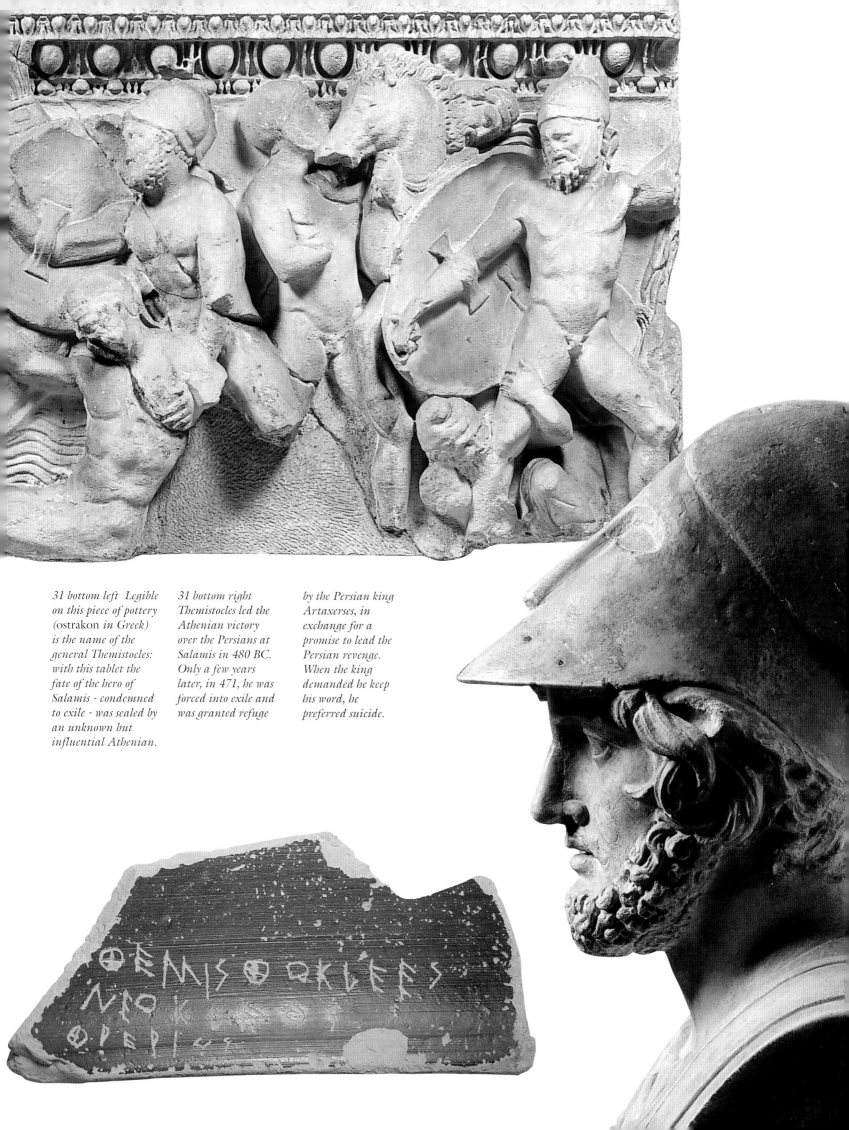

31 bottom left Legible on this piece of pottery (ostrakon *in Greek*) is the name of the general Themistocles: with this tablet the fate of the hero of Salamis - condemned to exile - was sealed by an unknown but influential Athenian.

31 bottom right Themistocles led the Athenian victory over the Persians at Salamis in 480 BC. Only a few years later, in 471, he was forced into exile and was granted refuge by the Persian king Artaxerses, in exchange for a promise to lead the Persian revenge. When the king demanded he keep his word, he preferred suicide.

Athens was the real winner of the Persian wars. Under the banner of the Delian League many cities of Asia Minor joined an economic and political alliance with Attica's capital. Within the city-state itself the democratic party gained control thanks to the determined efforts of new figures.

Most prominent amongst them was Pericles, an aristocrat converted to the "people's cause": he was the prime mover of the scheme to build the Acropolis, with the monumen-

tal Parthenon reflecting the political identity of the Athens.

From the Athens of the classical period came a burst of new ideas and amazing artistic talents: a phenomenon that rarely took place in history. The names of its protagonists - Aeschylus, Sophocles, Phidias, Herodotus, Aristophanes, Thucydides – say it all.

Then, just after the glory came the breakdown.

32 bottom right The transformation of Athens by Pericles, seen here in an idealized portrait, was part of a political and cultural scheme aimed at hegemony. But the monumental building works on the Acropolis and in the city center also produced major economic benefits.

33 bottom right Excavated from the rock of the Acropolis was the theater of Dionysus. In the front tier of the auditorium were 67 places reserved for magistrates and priests; the city' poorest citizens were in any case admitted free. Greek tragedy boasted in 5th-century Athens the three great writers Aeschylus (who had fought at Marathon), Sophocles and Euripedes.

32 left This 19th-century print shows what Phidias's colossal chryselephantine statue of Athena, in the Parthenon, may actually have looked like; this work of art, presumably a perfect masterpiece, disappeared from the temple in the Byzantine period.

32-33 It took Pericles only 20 years, 450-430 BC, to make the city of Athens unique in the world. "When our city has met its obligations on the battlefield - Pericles reportedly told the Athenians (according to Plutarch) - should it not dedicate its available resources to initiatives that will produce eternal glory once completed, and tangible prosperity while in progress?" The result of his politics can be seen in this 19th-century reconstruction which shows Athens at the high of its power.

34 bottom left Philip – seen here in an idealized bust – became King of Macedonia in 359 BC. Educated in Greece, the father of Alexander the Great was a cultured, eloquent man and a great strategist. Thanks to his military strength and diplomatic skills he conquered the whole of Greece in the space of a few years.

34-35 In the spring of 334, two years after the death of his father Philip, the young Alexander landed near Troy. After performing a sacrifice in honor of Achilles, he attacked the Persian army on the river Granicus and started his conquest of Asia. The Macedonian charge is immortalized in the 19th-century print reproduced here.

The disastrous conflict with Sparta, the Peloponnesian War, followed by a plague that sapped the lifeblood of Athens, and carried off Pericles himself, political and tactical errors dealt the final blows to Athens and its century of enlightenment. First Sparta, then Thebes became "mistress" of the Greek cities. Soon the 5th century was over, the 4th was well under way and Athens was just raising her head again when the Macedonians appeared on the scene.

Philip of Macedon had set his mountainous northern kingdom in order and founded an army skilled in rapid and effective techniques of attack. But he relied first and fore-

35 top Alexander carried out practically unequalled exploits and left a fabled image to history. This intense portrait was by Leocare.

35 bottom The bas-relief of Xanthos shows hoplites besieging a well-defended enclosure wall.

most on a popular sentiment that has always produced results: the desire to be part of a strong and united nation. In 338 BC he won the day at Chaeronea, defeating the Athenians. In Corinth he then promoted a Pan-Hellenic league, allowing the cities to retain their autonomy formally provided they acknowledged the authority of the king of Macedonia.

Philip was dead before he succeeded in extending his kingdom beyond the borders of Greece; it was instead his son, Alexander, who set off to conquer the lands of Greece's age-old enemies, the Persians. He routed them first out of Asia Minor, then Egypt, where he founded Alexandria, the Hellenistic city par excellence; lastly he attacked Persia itself, before marching on as far as the Indus. He died at the age of only 33, in 323 BC, after ten years spent fighting on a single campaign.

His empire was divided among the Greek kingdoms of the East, under various dynasties. Controlled by Macedonian kings, descendants of companions of Alexander the Great, Greece itself entered a period of decline. Trade routes, and cultural developments too, gave weakened Greece a wide berth.

36 This Hermes by Praxiteles, displayed in the Archaeological Museum in Olympia, is an outstanding example of the level of maturity attained in Greek sculpture: the observer senses the artist's compelling desire to capture natural beauty and hold it for posterity. Praxiteles also was the author of rules on the position of the body in statuary art.

37 left The Venus of Milo is considered to exemplify the culminating point of Hellenistic art. This celebrated statue was made by an unknown 2nd-century sculptor.

37 right Another portrait of Aphrodite, this time a 1st-century AD copy of a Hellenistic original. Here the uncommon sense of immediacy implicit in the pose reveals a masterly rendering that already verges on decadence.

In 214 BC the Romans set foot on the Greek peninsula for the first time, in the first of three Macedonian Wars: less than 50 years later, in 168 BC, the Roman consul Paulus Aemilius conquered Macedonia and annexed the new province of Greece. From then on the history of Greece became intermingled with that of Rome: freedmen, philosophers and politicians emigrated to the new capital and became part of its establishment. Greece itself was the scene of battles waged within the empire: Pharsalus, Philippi, Actium are geographical landmarks attesting to Rome's power, sites of battles fought by Caesar and his successors. Flaws in the "pax romana" began to appear in 200 AD with the invasion of the Goths but it was Christianity, imposed as the state

religion by Constantine, that destroyed the very foundations of Hellenism. The division of the Roman Empire into two, in the last decade of the 3rd century, and a further wave of Goth invaders, signalled the demise of Roman Greece.

Greek was the language of the Eastern Roman Empire; its capital, Byzantium (the new name of Constantinople), had originally developed as a colony of Megara. In a certain respect, however, Greece was no more than a "secondary province" of the empire, which stretched right across the southern shores of Italy, the whole of North Africa as far as Asia

Minor. The Greek peninsula itself became easy prey for the many waves of barbarians who descended from the northeast. After Attila's invasion in 447, it was over-run several times by hordes of Huns, and Slavic tribes who rampaged the length and breadth of the country into areas like Epirus (where, even today, people talk with a guttural inflection typical of the Slav languages) and Macedonia. The court of Byzantium was too busy confronting a stronger enemy, to concern itself with the Greek province and its problems.

In 638, only six years after the death of Mohammed, the armies

38 top right This bronze statue of a nameless figure, found on the island of Delos, dates to 100 BC. It shows how the traditional Greek ideal of beauty - in its Hellenistic interpretation - was successfully integrated with the realistic, graphic approach of Roman art.

38 bottom left The relief on the arch of Galerio in Salonika shows a war scene at the gates of a city. Among the figures, the outline of a battle-elephant can be seen.

The arch stands on Via Egnatia, a large arterial road built by the Romans from the Ionian Sea to the east over the mountainous province of the empire.

39 top left The consul Metellus enters Athens. Not until the victory of the consul Paulus Aemilius over the Macedonian dynasty, at Pydna, was the "Greek province" annexed to the Roman Empire, in 146 BC.

39 bottom right After pushing west for centuries from the steppes of Mongolia, the Huns crossed the empire's frontiers along the Danube and Rhine in 375 AD. Waves of Germanic peoples flocked into the empire's territories in

search of refuge, but eventually the dreaded Huns arrived. And after the foray by Attila (seen here in an "imaginary" portrait by an unknown Italian artist) in 447, Greece was periodically raided and despoiled.

of Islam had conquered Persia and Palestine and were preparing to invade Egypt and seize Alexandria, the real center of trade and culture in the southern Mediterranean.

The Muslim army swept like wildfire across northern Africa, encountering populations that had no love for the Byzantine emperor or, especially, for his governors. In 670 the Arabs were at the gates of Constantinople: a seven-year seige ended with the withdrawal of the Prophet's troops. But paradoxically these very marauders on horseback who had set the Orient ablaze were the men who preserved and passed down the great books of classical culture, starting from Aristotle.

Eventually, the invasion of the Greek peninsula by the Slavs became inevitable. The Byzantine empire had to live with the threat or reality of invasion for several centuries, until the end of the period of the iconoclast controversy when it was under both military and cultural attack. Not until 864 AD, when the Slavs converted to the Orthodox religion,

did things calm down. But then a new threat arose, this time from the Bulgars: first, led by their tsar Simeon, they conquered Thrace and Macedonia; later, under Samuel, they extended their nation's power into Thessaly, until overwhelmed in 1014 by Basil II Bulgaroctonus ("killer of Bulgars").

At the end of the first millenium great upheavals were taking place throughout the Mediterranean area: first as a consequence of the crusade led by Godfrey of Bouillon which touched much of the Byzantine kingdom, then with the expansionist ambitions of the Normans and Venetians.

41 bottom Depicted in this miniature, on a manuscript written in Greek and entitled Oracle of Leo the Wise, is the "vacant throne of Constantinople," an allegory referring to a victory over the Ottomans by emperor Leo, son of Basil and Eudocia.

40-41 Byzantine Greece was not spared invasions: countless Slav tribes, and particularly Bulgars, made forays into the peninsula. The illustration from a medieval text reproduced here shows one of many fruitless seiges laid by the invaders to Salonika.

40 bottom left The miniature reproduced here, from a French medieval manuscript, shows Godfrey of Bouillon, commander of the Christian armies of the Crusade, giving orders to his knights.

41 top In the mid-9th century the marriage took place between Basil I and Eudocia Ingerina. The bride's finery and the architecture testify to the wealth and strength of the Byzantine empire, which had by now separated its church from that of Rome.

42 top left This
exquisitely executed
picture shows the
naval battle of Milos,
where huge Turkish
and Venetian fleets
were in combat. It
comes from the
Report on the
Manoeuvres of the
Ottoman Armies.

42-43 At Lepanto the
West won the day with
a hurriedly gathered
and little trained
army. Firearms were
decisive in the outcome
of the battle: it was
much simpler to
quickly master use of
the rudimentary
muskets of those days
than to shoot arrows
with precision.

*42 bottom left
Illustrated in*
Turkish Memoirs *is
another episode of the
war between the
Ottoman empire and
Venice: the capture of
the tower on the
island of Lemnos,
only a short way from
the Turkish coast.
This 17th-century
manuscript was
produced in the
Iranian style of
Ottoman
miniaturists.*

*43 right On the
island of Rhodes the
monastic order of the
Knights of St. John
withstood the assaults
of the Ottoman
empire for two
centuries. Nevertheless
in 1522 Suleyman II
began a six-month
seige that compelled
them to leave the
island for good. As
documented by this
miniature, the
Turkish troops vastly
outnumbered the
defenders.*

With the beginning of the XI century the Serenissima republic began to make its commercial and military strength felt further and further east: castles appeared in increasing numbers on the islands and shores of Greece, particularly after Byzantium asked the Venetians for help in fighting the Norman Roger II who, from his Sicilian kingdom, had succeeded in conquering Corfu and Attica.
The superpowers of that period turned Greece into a chessboard, and the winner of each game helped themselves to the spoils: the prosperous centers of trade went to Venice; in 1200 the Frankish princes took over the kingdom of Salonika, the duchy of Athens and the principality of the Morea; Byzantium subjugated the despotate of Epirus to the Greek ruler Michael Comnenus. At this time the real capital of Byzantine Greece was Mystra, center of a cul-

westwards. As a province of the Ottoman empire Greece was subject to a feudal system not dissimilar to the one that previously existed under Byzantine rule. The Muslim religion of the Ottoman Turks did not enforce mass conversions, for adults at least, but catechism was compulsory for children and military service for youths. Taxes were payable to collectors often of Bulgarian or Albanian origin, a fact that sowed the seeds of the tension ever-present in relations between the various Balkan peoples. The peasants who cultivated the most fertile land were reduced to share-croppers or even slaves; the Greeks were left the mountainous regions and areas under the supervision of Orthodox monasteries. A series of uprisings shook the country in the late 16th and early 17th century, and in the mountainous regions furthest inland, whose affairs the Turks had little interest in managing, a rudimental local Greek administration took over, protected by bands of thieves and brigands (*klephtai*).

tural revival that overshadowed Constantinople and its civilization. A new interest in Plato's philosophies developed - partly as a reaction to medieval Aristotelism - and eventually spread to Italy and the rest of Europe, sparking off the Renaissance. Another major cause of these new developments was the dispersion of intellectuals after the fall of Constantinople to the Turks (1453).

The Ottoman conquest of Greece was in fact already in progress in 1400, with the Turks occupying first the north - Thrace, Thessaly, Macedonia, Epirus, then Salonika and lastly Athens, which fell in 1460; the Peloponnese and the island of Aegina remained in Venetian hands. The simultaneous influence of Turks and Venetians created a situation of instability that persisted until 1571 when the historic battle of Lepanto put a stop to Ottoman expansion

Early in the 18th century the Turks also conquered the Peloponnese, until then under Venetian rule. But another century passed – with the Ottoman empire continuing its process of gradual disintegration – before the awakening of a national consciousness among the Greeks, incited by the rest of Europe where there was strong support for the Greek cause. Philhellenism was not only inspired by the cultural movement led by liberals and Romantic poets, among them the already famous Lord Byron, who set sail for Greece to fight against the Turks: close political affinities existed, for example, between the Italian Risorgimento and

the support of the Pasha of Egypt, and the war of independence became an international conflict in which the great powers, France, Russia and Great Britain, declared war on the Ottoman empire and defeated the Turks at Navarino in 1827. These same powers chose the king who was to rule after the assassination of Kolokotronis, the Russo-Greek diplomat who had directed the last phase of the independence process. Otho of Bavaria thus came to occupy the royal palace in Athens, hurriedly built after the capital was transferred to Attica's small but prestigious city, symbol of a classical Greece it was hoped might be renewed. This solution hardly suited the Greeks: from Bavaria the king brought administrators, courtiers, even a garrison of Bavarian troops; the economic situation was critical; the new country was too small (it was comprised solely of the Peloponnese, the Cyclades and half of mainland Greece). Resentment among the population continued to grow, fuelling the cause of the rebirth of a Byzantine empire. The year 1843 saw the first of the ten military coups that have been the bane of the political life of modern Greece, almost to the present day.

In theory Otho was a constitutional monarch but in practice he held almost absolute power. Discontent among intellectuals and students increased when he supported Austria in the Italian war of independence. The revolt spread and in 1862 the king was deposed. There being no valid alternatives to bring the crisis to an end, the three protecting powers eventually selected a candidate to fill the vacant throne of Athens: the young George William of Denmark took the title "George I of the Hellenes" (his predecessor had been "king of Hellas"). This was considered a "step forward" that was justified with the cession of the Ionian Islands to Greece by Great Britain. A revised constitution based on a parliamentary system was accepted by the new king, but political crises and changes of government often occurred between 1864 and 1908.

the Greek struggle for independence, and the opposite shores of the Ionian Sea witnessed frequent comings and goings of political refugees and émigrés from the two countries.

A now-legendary skirmish marked the start of the war of independence. It took place on a bridge over the river Alamana (and is recalled in countless folk songs, including later ones about the resistance movement). Near Lamia, in central Greece, a Turkish army patrol came across a band of men-at-arms (*armatoloi*), the local militia at the service of the sultan. This small group led by Athanasios Diakos, an unfrocked Orthodox priest, was already involved in the fight for independence. In the ensuing clash the Greeks fought – so the story goes – like lions but the Turks were more numerous. Diakos was beaten, taken prisoner and shot in Lamia's main square.

The rebellion got under way in earnest in 1821. Supported by the Orthodox clergy it quickly spread through the peninsula, establishing a stronghold in the Peloponnese. The Turks enlisted

45

46-47 *This photograph from* Illustrazione Italiana *shows King George only a few minutes before his assassination in Salonika, in 1913. During his reign Greece had become an increasingly liberal state, although under close supervision from the Great Powers. It also regained many of its territories in the north: Thrace, Epirus and the Ionian Islands.*

46 bottom *Rebellious troops march through the streets of Salonika during the uprising of 1916, instigated by Eleutherios Venizelos, prime minister under George I. Venizelos set up a military government and overthrew Constantine I, a fierce opponent of liberal reform.*

The Cretan uprising of 1897 persuaded the king to embark on a conflict with Turkey; it ended, however, with the Greeks being defeated on the northern borders of their state and obliged to return several border territories. In 1910, after yet another coup, Elefterios Venizelos became prime minister and, through an alliance with the other Balkan states, he succeeded in doubling his country's territory in the space of four years. Epirus, Macedonia and Crete too were annexed to Greece. The new government instituted a liberal state after the long inertia-plagued years of monarchy.

In 1913 King George I was assassinated in Salonika and his successor, Constantine, moved towards an al-

47 bottom right Venizelos was certainly Greece's most prominent politician in the period between the 19th and the 20th century. He was a point of reference for the army, for decades its only organized interlocutor on the political scene; he was also the instigator of liberal reforms. A skilled diplomat and shrewd statesman, Venizelos nonetheless remains a contradictory figure.

47 left This picture was taken in 1913, during the Balkan War. Greek troops are advancing towards Ioannina, capital of Epirus: they have occupied positions along the road and take cover while waiting for the order to attack.

47 top right An official portrait of King Constantine, before his abdication. Replaced by his son Alexander in 1917, he returned to the throne in 1920 after his successor's death and remained king until 1922, the year in which the defeat at the hands of the Turks forced him to abdicate.

liance with Germany, at the very time of the outbreak of World War I. But the Venizelos government sided instead with the Triple entente of France, Great Britain and Italy: forced to resign, Venizelos led a military arising and eventually replaced Constantine with the young Alexander. At the end of World War I Greece sat at the victors' conference table and did its utmost to secure the re-acquisition of Greek territories in Asia Minor. In 1919

Greek troops occupied Smyrna but the Turkish army, led by Mustafa Kemal (later called Ataturk) reconquered the city: the dream of a Great Greece was crushed as the city was burnt to the ground and the remaining Greeks massacred. The ensuing disastrous Greco-Turkish war ended with an agreement for the exchange of populations: about 400,000 Turks then living in Greece emigrated to Asia Minor, while no fewer than 1,500,000 Greeks were forced to settle in a "foreign" homeland. A social and economic catastrophe that was first and foremost, a disaster for humanity, was described in an amazingly vivid way by a reporter named Ernest Hemingway.

Meanwhile, 1920 had seen the death of the young King Alexander, replaced by his father, which was unusual. The crisis in Asia Minor led to the abdication of the king in 1922 and victory for a republican government. This was a period of total instability, marked by a series of coups d'état and temporarily ended by Venizelos' return, from 1928 to 1932. Eventually, after the rule of a military junta, the monarchy was restored in 1935. In 1936, under pressure from King George II, the Greek parliament appointed Iannis Metaxas as prime minister, thereby introducing a regime

aligned, in Europe, with those of Mussolini, Hitler and Franco. But the decision in favor of an alliance with Fascism and Nazism did not save the Greeks from invasion by the Italians and Germans. On October 28th 1940, the Italian ambassador in Athens, Grazzi, handed Metaxas an Italian order to the effect that Greece be annexed to Italy. Metaxas refused, and three days later Italian invaders landed on the Ionian coast, where they very quickly became bogged down in a hard, slow advance over the mountains of Epirus. In gruelling trench warfare the Greek troops – as badly organized and equipped as the Italian Fascists – gradually lost ground. Then, in April 1941, the Germans also attacked Greece, via Yugoslavia and Albania. Although the Nazi invasion sealed the fate of Greece, the occupying army's problems were far from over: the first parachute regiments dropped on Crete were exterminated, and fierce fighting continued all over the peninsula.

49 top The German offensive against Greece started on April 6th 1941; the Greek forces surrendered on April 24th. Fighting continued only in Crete. Here we see the effects of German bombing raids of May 1941 on the town of Chanià.

49 bottom At Larisa, in central Greece, Fieldmarshall List consults his plan of battle. The German army intervened in Greece only after the abortive Italian offensive, launched in October 1940: the Italians were halted by fierce resistance from Greek troops, and forced to winter in the mountains of Epirus.

In 1941 Greek resistance was practically non-existent: there was only one major incident, when Manolis Glezos lowered the flag with the swastika flying from the Parthenon. The following year the EAM (National Liberation Front) was founded by the Greek Communist Party, with the support of the trade unions and other left-wing groups, socialists included.

Early in 1942 EAM established a guerrilla force known as the ELAS (National Popular Liberation army). In the winter of 1941-42, the Greek population paid a cruel price for the war and their defeat: no fewer than 300,000 people died of hunger. By the end of 1942 and throughout 1943 the people were resorting to more than passive noncooperation: in Athens. Alone among the occupied capitals, 200,000 people (out of a total one million inhabitants) took to the streets in a mass protest against the deportations and hard labor.
But the resistance movement was not only strong in Athens.
Rural areas were now no longer safe for Italian and German troops: on March 7th 1943 the Italian garrison at Grevena, a provincial town in northern Greece, was attacked and defeated by an improvised troup of peasants. The Italians were not the only ones to withdraw. By the end of 1943 the entire Hellenic peninsula –

50 left German tanks roll through the streets of Kozani, in northern Greece. Armed resistance against the occupying forces really got underway in 1942, from hideouts deep in the mountains.

50-51 A contingent of German troops crosses the canal dug in the isthmus of Corinth to provide a shorter sea route between the gulf of Patras and the port of Athens. Smaller boats, less deep of draft, were the only ones that could be used on the canal.

pation a Greek government in exile, led by the king and a center-right executive, was formed in Cairo. In 1942 another resistance movement, the EDES (Greek Democratic National army), was set up under the command of General Zerzas with the support of the monarchy and the British. The two guerrilla forces undertook several acts of sabotage together, including the destruction of the railway bridge over the river Gorgopotamos, which stopped military supplies reaching German and Italian troops between the north and Athens. But political and organizational differences between the two created a precarious partnership that soon collapsed. Meanwhile, on the European war front, the defeat of the Axis was fast approaching. And with the formation by Colonel Grivas of bands of partisan-chasing collaborators, the first signs were seen of a conflict that eventually turned into civil war.

51 top An air squadron drops crack troops for the battle of Crete. With the arrival of German parachutists and the resistance of Greek soldiers determined to hold key positions on the island, the struggle for control of the eastern Mediterranean entered its crucial phase.

51 bottom The Nazi flag is raised on the Parthenon, immediately after its capture. A few months later the newly organized Greek resistance removed the swastika from the Acropolis. This was their first subversive action and the gesture had strong symbolic significance. The young Manolis Glezos was arrested, tortured and deported for having torn down the flag of the occupying army.

except for Athens, Salonika and the main communication routes – was in the hands of the Liberation army, ELAS, led by its charismatic *kapetanios* Aris Veluchiotis, a Communist not greatly loved by Moscow and a maverick in the eyes of the Greek party's leadership.

In the spring of 1943 ELAS could count on 5,000 men; five months later the ranks of the Liberation army had swelled to 40,000 freedom fighters enlisted throughout the rural areas of Greece, aided in their struggle by EAM agitators in the cities.

The existence of liberated areas run by ELAS administrators along egalitarian and collectivist lines, did not save Greece from the horrors of Nazi occupation: in 1943 and 1944 55,000 Jews from Salonika were sent to concentration camps. Of the 68,000 Greek Jews arrested and deported to Germany, only 2,000 survived.

Immediately after the German occu-

in which Stalin had agreed to exclude Greece from the Soviet bloc in return for Rumania). At the same time the Communist Party was detaching itself – in more ways than one – from the partisan forces in the mountains. In October 1944 the Germans withdrew from Greece and, within a few days, the British General Scobie had entered Athens. But peace was not yet at hand. The provisional government was bitterly divided, the Communist Party demanding greater room for maneuver: on December 3rd the police fired on left-wing demonstrators in Athens, barricades appeared in working-class districts and British guns fired on the city from its outskirts. The battle of Athens was a seige that ended only after six weeks of house-to-house combat.

At the peace conference held in February 1945 ELAS accepted to disarm and elections were held, won by the royalist party. A plebiscite on the king's return brought George II back to his Athens palace, with 69% of the votes. But the civil war was still not over, especially in the countryside: death squads were paid for the heads of communists, and EAM/ELAS bands continued to control certain towns and mountain areas. Not only was Greece split, so was the Communist Party itself. Party officials in Athens received orders from

In 1944, with the country still occupied by the Nazis, EAM's National Liberation Committee called free elections, and more than a million Greeks voted for a national government, under the German unseeing eyes. In May the Allies assigned to Georgios Papandreou, a former Liberal minister with the pre-Metaxas government, the task of forming a government of national unity to replace the one set up in exile in Cairo. At the conference organized in Lebanon, Papandreou obtained the Communist Party's agreement to join the new coalition, as well as recognition of Greece's international status within the Atlantic alliance (the Communists too were well aware of the contents of the treaty signed at Yalta,

52 top *The Nazis withdrew from Greece in October 1944. Here we see the enthusiastic welcome received by British troops in Xilocastro.*

52 bottom *This very unusual picture is of a group of anti-Nazi German resistance fighters, who had joined the Greek pro-communist resistance movement, EAM-ELAS.*

53 top *Here the troops that fought against the communist guerrillas parade beneath the Acropolis in Athens, at the end of the civil war.*

53 bottom *This photograph of Georgios Papandreu, the man behind the Lebanon agreement, was taken outside the Royal Palace after he had sworn in the presence of King Paul I.*

Moscow to disarm. The directives printed on the front page of the party newspaper spoke clearly: no food nor refuge for Veluchiotis, the partisan leader still fighting in the mountains. Finally trapped in a mill with a few of his men, Veluchiotis was captured and killed by a band of headhunters: his own head was displayed the following day in Lamia's main square.

The last pocket of resistance in Epirus was crushed on Mount Grammos: the British bombed the few remaining guerrilla groups defending positions close to the Albanian border.

On this occasion napalm was used for the first time in Greece. The great escape then began: an estimated 100,000 people – Communists, Socialists but also freedom fighters with no party affiliations – crossed the border into neighboring communist countries; far from receiving a triumphant welcome they suffered the fate of renegades. On the most desolate Greek islands concentration camps opened their doors to leftwingers, and democrats too.

In Athens, from 1945 to 1952 governments came and went, with an average lifespan of 150 days. A temporary "solution" was found when yet another strong man entered the political arena: General Papagos, who had been in command of troops that defeated both the Italians and - later - Communist rebels. After him came a succession of right-wing governments, several headed by the conservative leader Konstantinos Karamanlis and the now-ageing Georgios Papandreou. Following the death of King Paul I and the accession to the throne of his son Constantine in 1964, there was a serious rift between Papandreou and the young king, mainly regarding control of the armed forces. In 1967, on the eve of elections that seemed likely to be won by the left, a group of army officers seized power. The elections

ment, death sentence – not executed – and continued torture shook public opinion in Greece and worldwide). But the Polytechnic beseiged by the army, the students killed in the fighting, the city's emotional involvement with the many wounded or forced to flee: all this had significant weakening effects on the regime. Papadopoulos was deposed and General Ghizikis took his place. Only a few months later, in July 1974, the junta tried to annex Cyprus, attempting to overthrow the government of Archbishop Makarios. The Turks reacted by sending their army to take over control of the island, and half of it was subsequently annexed to Turkey.

55 bottom right At the 1975 trial which was the last act of the long dictatorship of the colonels, the accused are seen seated on the right, facing the jury that condemned Papadopoulos (first on the left, by the guard) to death. His sentence was commuted to life imprisonment. He died in June 1999

were banned and a witch-hunt to seek out Communists began: the concentration camps, never closed since the end of the civil war, were filled with thousands of people (6,000 in Yaros alone); torture became the normal way of dealing with opposition. Leading the junta was Colonel Papadopoulos; although the monarchy had not initially opposed the coup, in December it led an abortive attempt to overthrow the regime. King Constantine then had no other option but exile. Georgios Papandreou died in 1968. His funeral brought huge crowds into the streets: hundreds of thousands of defiant Athenians shouted in unison "Stand up, old man, look how many of us there are," as they displayed their opposition to the military regime. But the following years saw the arrest of dissenters, a ban on free political parties and trade unions, police controls, censorship, enforcement in schools of use of a classical language invented in the 19th century to encourage continuity with the Athens of Pericles. Not until 1973, when students in the capital occupied the Polytechnic, did the opposition openly challenge the regime again. There had been isolated incidents, bomb attacks on statues of the previous century's numerous tyrants, a dramatic attempt to assassinate Papadopoulos by a young officer, Alexander Panagoulis (his imprison-

55 top left General Papagos, a leading figure of the civil war, hoped to become the strongman of governments that followed the Papandreu legislature. He succeeded in 1952, winning the elections with explicit aid from the American embassy.

55 top right In July 1965 the police staged an attack on participants at a rally in support of the Georgios Papandreou, then prime minister. Later that year, due to differences of opinion with King Constantine, Papandreou was dismissed.

56-57 The meeting of
Nea Dimokratia filled
the squares of Athens
on the occasion of early
elections in June 1985.
The elections signalled
the return to strength
of the party led by
Mitsotakis.

56 bottom left
Costantino
Karamanlis, the
leader of the extreme
right, was appointed
Prime Minister in
1955 in place of
Marshall Papagos.
After the long
dictatorial regime of
the Army, he returned
to power in 1974 with
his new party, Nea
Dimokratia, and was
later appointed
president of the
republic for two terms,
until 1995.

56 bottom right
Portrayed with his wife
at Greek Easter 1990,
Costantino Mitsotakis
celebrated his
appointment as Prime
Minister in the same
year, the position he
held for 3 years.
A politician since
1946, Mitsotakis
became secretary of
Karamanlis' party in
1984.

57 top In 1989,
scandal brought down
the Socialist
government and
swept the right to
power in the summer
elections. The
Panhellenic Socialist
Party managed to get
back to power in 1993
under the leadership
of Andrea
Papandreou.

The junta fell on July 23rd 1974: within
an hour of the news that the colonels
had been deposed, Athens was thronging with rejoicing Greeks. Konstantinos
Karamanlis, the former leader of the
right, was called to guide the transition;
a referendum held in December abolished the monarchy and banished the
king for good. Among the politicians
who returned from exile was Papandreou's son Andreas, a former member
of PAK, a non-communist left-wing
movement formed to oppose the junta.
Back in Athens, he founded the Pan-
Hellenic Socialist movement (PASOK).
The right rallied under the banner of the
New Democracy Party of Karamanlis,
whereas the Center Union Party, once
led by Georgios Papandreou, reasserted

57 center Supporters of the PASOK were disappointed by the elections in 1985, 1986 and 1989 when the majority was led by Nea Dimokratia. This state of affairs remained until 1993 when Andrea Papandreou led the party to power for the last time before handing it over to Kostas Simitis.

57 bottom The socialist Kostas Simitis has taken on the responsibility to ensure Greece to maintain its democracy, strengthen its position in the European Union so that the country would finally leave behind its sorrowful experiences of the past.

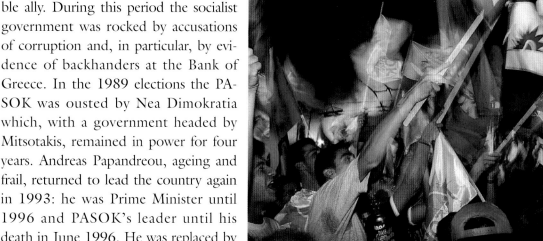

ble ally. During this period the socialist government was rocked by accusations of corruption and, in particular, by evidence of backhanders at the Bank of Greece. In the 1989 elections the PASOK was ousted by Nea Dimokratia which, with a government headed by Mitsotakis, remained in power for four years. Andreas Papandreou, ageing and frail, returned to lead the country again in 1993: he was Prime Minister until 1996 and PASOK's leader until his death in June 1996. He was replaced by Kostas Simitis, a young economist who grew up during the period the Socialists were in power. Simitis was Prime Minister for 8 years and, in turn, was replaced in 2004 by Kostas Karamanlis, a member of the conservative party. The country, which joined the European Union in 1981, adopted the euro as its official currency in 2001. The standard of living has improved dramatically in Greece in recent years. Even the age-old rivalry with the Turks has dropped off, above all after the disastrous earthquakes that struck Turkey and Greece in August-September 1999 and left thousands of victims, demonstrating the need for collaboration between the two countries. The country's development was eloquently demonstrated in 2004 when Athens hosted the Olympic Games, unanimously considered a resounding success. This was the best opportunity for the Greeks to proudly repropose the prestigious traditions of ancient Greece, showing the world the new achievements of this small but great nation.

its position. The first Karamanlis government held a referendum that turned Greece into a republic. It also set about finding a non-traumatic way for the junta and its administration to settle their outstanding accounts: three of the colonels (including Papadopoulos) considered guilty of the most heinous crimes were condemned to death, but the sentences were never executed. The 1981 elections swept Andreas Papandreou's PASOK party to power, the first left-wing government in Greece's history. The charismatic socialist leader had the task of leading Greece through radical changes to its structures; at the same time a very cool foreign policy – at least apparently – was adopted towards the USA, which had always looked upon Turkey as a more sta-

58 top Syntagma Square is the capital's business district, as well as its political heart. Lining all four sides are foreign consulates, headquarters of prominent companies, offices of airlines. But expanses of tables set up by bars and cafés also contribute to the general hustle and bustle.

58 center The neoclassical Academy is one of the imposing buildings erected during Athens' golden age, immediately after the city was made capital, in the 19th century. Some of the finest architects of that period were involved in the urban planning scheme, designed with Parisian lines.

59 top right The old royal palace, in central Sintagma Square, is now the seat of parliament. The square has witnessed important events in the country's political history, from the mass demonstration against the Nazis in 1943 to the closing rallies of electoral campaigns under the present democracy.

58 bottom A guard of honor stands by the monument to the fallen, in Syntagma Square. The evzones wear the traditional costume of northern Greece: short baggy trousers, a kind of fez and shoes with big pompoms on the toes.

58-59 About one third of the Greek population lives in the vast metropolitan area formed by Athens and its port, Piraeus. The city and suburbs stretch across a vast plain, from the slopes of Mount Parnis to the sea; the old center is instead concentrated between the two hills of the Acropolis and Likavitos.

59 top left Piraeus, the largest port in Greece and one of the most important in the Mediterranean, has a series of natural harbors where pleasure boats are moored. After dark things get lively in this waterfront city, with its restaurants and tavernas where traditional music is played.

S prawling across a vast plain wedged between the mountains of Attica and the Saronic Gulf is the modern city of Athens. Little more than a century ago a far different scene greeted visitors to the region: olive groves were still abundant and on the slopes of the surrounding hills, now swallowed up by metropolitan Athens, were the famous white Pentelic marble quarries. These provided the stone used to create the great monuments of the Acropolis and, twenty-three centuries later, friezes that adorn the most important buildings erected in the 19th century. The initial core of Athens, now a major capital, was a small area lying between the flattened rock on which the Parthenon stands and the cone-shaped Likavitos, two soaring landmarks in the very center of the city. The urban expansion of Greece's capital took place in several phases. Architecturally speaking, it got off to a good start. The initial city plan created quarters with wide thoroughfares, modelled on the Parisian boulevards. The second phase came about as a consequence of repeated waves of immigration of the Greeks from Asia Minor, and internal population movement. Suburbs developed haphazardly all around the old city, linked to the center by highways. Viewed from the air, modern Athens appears to have no limits. Emerging from a sea of buildings are the gleaming white mass of the Parthenon and the hill of Likavitos; the gardens by the royal palace are the only eye-catching patch of greenery

60 top This ornate, almost baroque statue of Athena represents the goddess in all her power and glory. It is a copy of the statue by Phidias, originally displayed in the Parthenon.

60 bottom Here we see the triumphant entrance to the Athenian Acropolis, with the Beule gate, the Propylaea and the temple of Athena Nike, goddess of victorious Attica. A visit to this unique archaeological and architectural site alone makes the journey to Greece worthwhile.

60-61 The Parthenon is concrete evidence of the Athenians' political aspirations: after the victory over the Persians Pericles hoped to unite the Greek world under Attica's leadership. This dream of establishing the hegemony of Athens and its democracy led to the construction of a temple visible from every corner of the city.

61 top The Erechtheum, with the most celebrated Caryatids carved by Alkamenes, a pupil of Phidias, is the temple dedicated to the heroes of the city. The monument has an essentially Ionic gracefulness, in contrast to the severe Doric power of the nearby Parthenon.

against the uniform color of the city. The situation of traffic and pollution, which was quite serious up to the Nineties, has gradually been improved by adopting regulations and parameters to lower emission levels. The 2004 Olympic Games also led to the redevelopment of entire areas of the capital and its infrastructures. A modern metropolis in every sense, Athens has worked specifically to maintain its timeless charm. Hardly surprisingly, the scenario is far different from that in the days of Pericles, Phidias and – if we stretch our imagination – Athena, powerful and capricious goddess and protectress of the city. All the same, Athens has its own special brand of appeal. Here people still value personal contact and find time to meet and chat (when not discussing things vociferously). The close-knit suburban fabric stems from the merging of countless ex-villages; the social structure of rural communities – focused, among other things, on the extended family – has survived and is jealously maintained. And it is the strengths and weaknesses of the peasant world that set Athens apart from the anonymity of other major European cities. The social scene is lively: there's room for about 400,000 customers in the myriad *cafenion* – focal point of convivial life in towns and cities all over Greece – of central Athens.

Old Athens is tiny, little more than the flat rock of the Acropolis with the

62 top left The Odeion of Herodes Atticus, at the foot of the Acropolis, is in an excellent state of preservation. This Roman theater can seat 5,000 and Athenians flock there on summer evenings to watch drama and music performances.

62 top right A number of important features differentiate the classical Greek arena from Roman theaters: for instance, the broad sweep of the stage and wider tiers to accommodate spectators. These characteristics are clearly evident in this photo, taken in the Dionysus theater.

62-63 Beside the Roman Agorà is the Tower of the Winds, with a water clock dating from the first century AD. Some of its eight faces, corresponding to the cardinal points, are decorated with figures personifying the winds.

*63 top The Stoà - or
Portico - of Attalos is
one of several
monuments entirely
reconstructed in the
Agorà. Now a
museum established by
the American School of
Archaeology in
Athens, it contains
statues and other finds
from the surrounding
excavations.*

*63 center The
Temple of Olympian
Zeus was built by
Hadrian - the
emperor and
philosopher who
owed so much to
Greece - as his
testimony to the
greatness of Greek
culture.*

*63 bottom Scattered
about the Acropolis
are pieces of columns
and capitals of the
various orders. With
no place found for
them in museums,
they form a kind of
"archaeology park"
scaled down to
human size.*

Parthenon at its center, and the characteristic quarter of Plaka, in the last few decades crowded with touristy shops and currently enjoying a general facelift. The early years of the 20th century produced the first evidence of the modern city that was to develop around this core. An ambitious city plan intended the new Athens to resemble the capitals of central Europe and especially Paris, with an urban layout hinged on the *leoforos*, "boulevards" that link the two main squares (Sintagma and Omonia) and then head north, to meet again beyond the hill of Likavitos. Along these main streets are neoclassical and modern buildings occupied by the city's important institutions: the vast National Archaeological Museum, boasting some of the world's very finest collections, and the Polytechnic, scene of the only uprising against the colonels' junta, in 1973; the Academy and the National Library, on Leoforos Venizelou; the American Embassy built along rationalist lines by Frank Lloyd Wright. These monuments, and the smart residential district of Kolonaki, on the slopes of Likavitos, are the most prominent features of present-day Athens.

City life radiates from Sintagma Square, smack in the center; this vast open space has always been a favorite place for pre-election rallies organized by the leading political parties. Overlooking the square is the imposing, neoclassical Greek Parliament building, once a royal palace. Tourists gather in front of it, several times a day, to watch

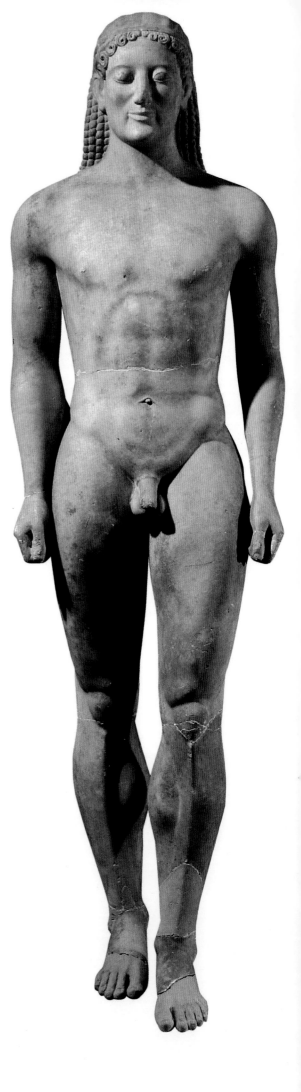

64 left The funerary stele of Aristion, carved by Aristokles, was erected in 510 BC. It became a symbol of the victory at Marathon where heavily outnumbered Athenian troops defeated the immense Persian army.

64 right The perfect forms of this boy - or kouros - from Anavyssos are classified according to the same orders used for architecture. This statue is Ionic and, dating to the 6th century BC, it exemplifies the Archaic style.

the changing of the guard "performed" by *evzones*, clad in their picturesque uniforms with the traditional short baggy trousers and sporting – in many cases – dashing uptwisted moustaches. Also overlooking Sintagma Square are the Hotel Grande Bretagne, its faded grandeur evocative of spies and intrigue (it was actually the Germans' headquarters during World War II), and the King George, with walls frescoed by eminent 19th century Greek artists.

At the rear of the Parliament building are the Ethnikòs Kipo, the National Gardens, a verdant oasis in the very center of the city. Inside the park stand the Zappion pavillions which were built in the 19th century in the architectural style of ancient Athens and host sports facilities; in summer the local people seek relief from the suffocating heat seated at the tables of an outdoor café; peacocks used to be seen here too, left free to wander among a variety of rare plants. Beyond Leoforos Olgas are Hadrian's Arch, of Roman origin, and the ancient Temple of Olympian Zeus, the largest sanctuary in Greece, constructed – so goes the legend – by Decaulion, the man who survived the Great Flood. From this point, following Leoforos Dhionisou Areopayitou, we come to the southern slope of the Acropolis, in the shadow of the massive Parthenon. At the base of the most celebrated rock in the ancient world are the theaters of Dionysus and Herodes Atticus; the latter, built in Roman times, now hosts a summer festival of ballet and drama that attracts the city's *glitterati*.

Turning off Leoforòs Dhionisou Areopayitou is the paved path that climbs up to the Acropolis. Grouped on this craggy limestone rock's flat summit (extending over an area of three hectares) are monuments of enormous significance for the history of Western art, philosophy and politics. As in ancient times, the Acropolis is entered beneath the colonnade of the Propylaea; at its side, across a piece of stony ground, is the small temple of Athena Nike, goddess of victory. From here the Sacred Way continues as far as the Parthenon, the unparalleled masterpiece created by the genius of Phidias and, metaphorically speaking, by the democratic principles of Pericles. North of this temple of temples stands the Erechtheum with the Caryatids, the six famous maidens who have supported the building's Ionic frieze for the last

65 *left* The so-called Moskophoros, *"calf-carrier," is one of the sculptures that strike most for its flowing lines and sense of movement, even if it is an outstanding example of the Archaic style, datable to 570 BC.*

65 *right Rivulets of water appear to trickle down the hair and dress of this lovely Archaic* kore *("maiden"), who holds an apple in her hand. The statue stands in the Acropolis Museum, famous for its collection of "stone girls" from antiquity.*

saries of the Turkish government and English visitors, on a pilgrimage in search of vestiges of antiquity. And what did these Romantic travellers hope to find among this motley collection of shops and stalls? They came to gaze in wonder at Pericles' brainchild, the temple constructed from Pentelic marble by the architect Ictinus and decorated by Phidias, the greatest artist of classical antiquity: a miracle of architectural equilibrium, encompassed by 46 Doric columns of slightly different height, their profile almost imperceptibly curved to correct the optical illusion that makes perfectly straight columns seem concave. Until 1801 the sculptures that adorned the pediment and metope – originally painted blue, red, yellow and green – could be admired in situ.

66 top left These young boxers convey very clearly the sense of realism that inspired Cycladic art, which had close ties with the art of Crete. The fresco was detached from a wall in an aristocratic dwelling on the acropolis in Santorini.

66 bottom right Conserved in the National Archaeological Museum is this portrait of a fisherman, from a frescoed wall in Akrotiri, on the island of Santorini. It is one of the finest and most vivid wall paintings to have survived from the 16th century BC.

twenty-five centuries. This exceptional vantage point affords a fine panorama of the city and, when weather conditions are right, Piraeus and the island of Salamina also come into view.

The Acropolis was not always held in such high regard: as late as the 19th century the Parthenon was surrounded by assorted shops, and it even served as a mosque, topped with a minaret, after being used as a Christian church of the Byzantine cult, between the 6th and 13th centuries, and subsequently a Catholic place of worship, under the city's Frankish rulers. The Turks even used the temple as a powder magazine and in 1687, when it was hit by Venetian canonfire, its ceiling was blown to pieces. At the foot of the rock the tiny quarter of Plaka contained all Athens then had to offer: a well-stocked bazaar, merchants' dwellings, a few inns providing rooms for emis-

66-67 La Parisienne
is a unique testimony
to the refinement of
the court and noble
ladies of Crete; it
owes its name to the
figure's elegant
hairstyle and pose.
The island's female

population clearly
enjoyed relative
freedom and
importance, with a
lifestyle far different
to that later
experienced by
women in Classical
Greece.

discuss everything from prices to politics, statues and monuments dedicated to the legendary heroes who, like the Athenian Theseus, were the cultural and religious nexus of the city. Extending around the ancient Agora is its modern equivalent, Plateia Monastiraki, the most authentically Athenian part of Plaka: in this old quarter an indisputable 'flea-market' atmosphere prevails, its bustling streets lined with countless junk-shops, antiques dealers and the like. There is also no shortage of cafés offering American-style breakfast, tiny hotels and reasonably priced tavernas packed at every hour with locals and tourists. In Monastiraki Square itself, beside the old and rather shabby station of the railway line connecting central Athens to Piraeus, we find a 1700s mosque and the Pantanassa, a 10th-century Byzantine church; it is commonly known as *monastiraki* (the "little monastery"), which explains where the square got its name from. Athenian churches are far from imposing: not a single place of worship in the city conveys the idea that the patriarch of Athens occupies a prominent place in the Orthodox church (and in fact the primate of Istanbul has a more prestigious office, symbolically at least, since the Orthodox religion does not recognize the authority of figures like the Pope). In effect Mitropolis, the cathedral, is a modern building, squeezed between Plaka and Sintagma, whereas the city's old main church, is a small ancient construction in Erma Street, which runs from Sintagma Square to the Plaka. The reduced dimensions of Athenian churches represented a discreet way of not disturbing neighboring mosques dur-

Later, thanks to Lord Elgin, British ambassador to the Sublime Porte and an amateur archaeologist, many pieces of Parthenon sculpture found their way to the British Museum in London, allowing English enthusiasts to admire Phidias' works without leaving their native shores.

After the war of independence the Greeks saw Athens as the symbol of their nation's ancient splendor: following the arrival of the new king of the Hellenes, the city of Pericles became a capital once more. The Acropolis was cleared of shanty-style dwellings and minarets and a master plan was developed for the new city, to be built in the surrounding plain, occupied for millennia by wandering herders and their flocks. The city created with the contributions of Europe's finest 19th

and early 20th century planners now radiates from the base of the Acropolis, beneath the gaze of constant throngs of tourists.

Upon descending the slopes of the Acropolis we can – for a while – delay returning to the modern world: there are further vestiges of ancient Athens on the hill of the Areopagus, once sacred to Ares. Even prior to the classical period this was the site of the Council of Nobles and the Judicial Court. A *leofòros* now separates it from the Hill of the Nymphs and from the Pnyx, a man-made hill once used as the meeting-place of the Athenians' democratic assembly. Continuing north we come to the Agora, the focal point of commercial life in ancient Athens: situated here were council halls, gymnasiums, porticoes where people gathered to

ing the long centuries of Ottoman rule. A further example, close by, is the tiny church of Ayia Dhinami, wedged into the modern piers of the Ministry of Education.

Beyond Monastiraki, to the north, is the commercial district that gravitates towards Omonia Square, the second largest in the city after Sintagma. This is the business heart of Athens; the political parties and newspapers have their headquarters in the vicinity, and there is a large covered market where city-dwellers go to buy the freshest fish in town. Little shops in this modern bazaar stock everything imaginable, from mountain herbs to 'alternative'

68 Shown here is the face of Poseidon - or possibly Zeus - as imagined by an unknown artist from the 5th century BC. Semi-precious stones were probably used for the missing eyes, to add a touch of realism.

69 left The bronze statue of a youth discovered off Antikythira could be described as a "baroque" version of

the classicism typical of the 4th century BC. According to one plausible interpretation, it represents Perseus holding the decapitated head of Medusa.

69 right Here we see part of a statue from the late classical period, dedicated to Hygiea. It was created by Skopas, great genius and innovator of late Classical art.

medicinal remedies. It is the ideal place to buy *mastika* – the breath-sweetening resin that was the European precursor of chewing gum – but you may chance on roots of the magical mandragora too. Unassuming architecture of the Sixties prevails in these streets, laid out in a regular sunburst pattern intersected by roads running parallel. Yet this is the liveliest part of the city, never overlooked by tourists for whom the focus of interest is nevertheless the National Archaeological Museum. This treasure house of Cycladic, Mycenaean and classical art is a city within a city, where visitors spend whole days admiring the naturalist frescoes of Santorini or the vast collection of Attic vases. From the environs of Omonia Square three important thoroughfares lead back to Sintagma: Stadhiou, Panepistimou and Akadhimias are the most representative streets of the modern city, bordered by the neoclassical buildings of the Greek Academy and National Library. Until after World War II the architecture of many buildings in the city center was influenced by an original and attractive

neo-Hellenic style; on top of roofs were *akroteria*, red terracotta heads believed to bring good luck, also used to adorn the temples of antiquity. Nowadays they are not hard to find in little antiques shops and even flea markets. Sad to say, there is now little evidence of the ambitious urban developments meant to provide Athens with a cityscape fitting for the great capital of liberated Greece. Even the upmarket residential district of Kolonaki, tucked between Leoforos Akadhimas and the slopes of Likavitos, was rebuilt in the Fifties and Sixties. All that remains of 19th century Athens are the suburbs of Kastri, Kifissia and Kessariani, on the northern outskirts. To find a real gem of Byzantine art we must travel almost 30 kilometers from central Athens, along the road to Eleusis, to the monastery of Dhafni. Erected on the spot where the sanctuary of Apollo Daphnephoros once stood, the building is undoubtedly the region's finest testimony to Byzantine architecture; embellishing its interior are splendid mosaics with the stern image of Christ in Majesty (*Pandokrator*).

The environs of Athens offer many places of archaeological interest or scenic appeal. Less than 70 kilometers from the city, along the coastal road that passes through Glifadha, Voula and Vouliagmeni, Athens' smart beach resorts, is Cape Sounion. Dominating the landscape, on a cliff high above the sea, is the most celebrated of the temples dedicated to Poseidon. Still following the coast, beyond the old industrial town of Lavrio, we come to the archaeological site of Brauron (some 100 kilometers from Athens): its temple, dedicated to Artemides, was erected to placate the goddess who, angered by the killing of a bear, sent a plague to torment the people of Attica.

Northeast of Athens, beyond the industrial district of Eleusis, are the remains of the sanctuaries of Demeter and Persephone, where the ritual ceremonies known as the Eleusinian Mysteries were performed. A further 70 kilometers on the road and we reach Thebes, on the agricultural plain of Boeotia; the modern town and surrounding area offer little beside the fame of the legendary king Oedipus. A speedy tour of the region should nonetheless not overlook – in springtime – the flowering of the Boeotian tulip, a species that grows only in this area. Undoubtedly worth a detour, however, is the monastery of Ossios Loukas, reached following an uphill route towards the Elikonas peaks (70 kilometers from Thebes in the direction of Livadia): its beautiful

11th-century buildings are noted for their very distinctive architecture, based on the interplay of materials and color, and a series of outstanding frescoes.

Delphi is now no more than 20 kilometers away. With the sea as its backdrop, the celebrated sanctuary clings to the slopes of Mount Parnassos, above the sacred plain with its clusters of olive groves: it is a sight not to be missed, one of the most stunning and representative places in Greece. A full day at least is needed to visit the Sacred Precinct of Apollo, the Marmaria, the Castalian spring and all the other sites once crowded with pilgrims who came to seek enlightenment from the Oracle. The often equivocal answers obtained from the Pythian priestess "possessed" by Apollo, required the sacrifice of animals. The power of Delphi was so great that, for reasons we would nowadays define as "territorial control," two Sacred Wars were fought over possession of the sanctuary.

As in ancient times Delphi is entered along the Sacred Way. The path skirts memorials and Treasuries – votive offerings erected here by the cities that participated in the pan-Hellenic spirit of the sanctuary – before reaching the Temple of Apollo, similar in size to the Parthenon. But the first noticed and now most prominent feature of the whole archaeological site is the Tholos: this rotunda, in the Marmaria area, was a temple dedicated to Athena.

72 top right Ioannina has maintained its oriental character intact. The photograph shows the fort of Ali Pasha of Tepeleni that dominates the citadel. At the start of the 19th century, Ali's power was so large that it worried even the Sultan in Constantinople who sent a military expedition. After 15 months of siege, Ioannina capitulated and the Pasha was put to death.

72-73 This view of the port and bay in Parga on the west coast of Greece is seen from the Venetian castle. The small island with the chapel is a famous image of mainland Greece. The town is surrounded by centuries-old olive trees and is one of the pleasantest places on the Ionian coast.

*E*pirus, Macedonia, Thessaly and Thrace are the four northern regions of mainland Greece, a part of the country fairly seldom included on international tourism circuits. Their mountains and plains hardly fit the conventional image of the Mediterranean country. Many of the little towns which characterize this area still look the way they did in the past, having resisted the urban development of the early Sixties. Still surviving in these regions are ecosystems of exceptional environmental value: forests of pine trees alternate with sheer cliffs and gorges among the highest in Europe, while beautiful mountains - now protected in national parks – offer the ideal habitat for bears.

The first port of call for most visitors arriving in northern Greece from Europe is Igoumenitsa. From here it is possible to head directly inland or continue southwards along the Epirot coast. Taking the latter option, Parga is the first place of historic and scenic interest encountered. In the old town narrow streets descend from the Venetian castle overlooking the two bays to the harbor. Some 30 kilometers south of Parga, along the coastal route, is the gorge of the Acheron, the river over which – according to Greek mythology – Charon ferried the souls of the dead to Hades. At the mouth of the river are the ruins of the Necromanteion, the sanctuary dedicated to the cult of the Dead, built in the 3rd century BC and destroyed by the Romans in 168 AD. Further south is the vast Amvrakikos

gulf where the fleets of Antony and Octavian met in 31 BC at the historic battle of Actium. Still testifying to Octavian's success are the ruins of Nikopolis, "Victory City." With its huge theater and stadium, Nikopolis is the largest Roman archaeological site on Greek territory. If we do not follow the route that runs from Igoumenitsa to Ioannina, the inland region of Epirus can be approached by heading north from the Amvrakikos gulf, towards Filipiadha. Along the valley of the Luros is the turning for Dodona, one of the first holy places in ancient Greece. The cult practised here centerd on the Oracle of Zeus which spoke to its priests through the rustling leaves of an oak tree shaking in the wind. Back on the main road, Ioannina – capital of Epirus – is not far. One of the best preserved towns in the Hellenic peninsula, it owes part of its Balkan atmosphere to the minarets of the fortified citadel overlooking the lake, and the huge storks' nests. The grey stone fortress, paved streets and the clusters of silversmiths also add a Slav touch to the old town: in effect Ioannina became Greek only in 1913. From the mosque of Aslan Aga, now a museum, are clearly visible Lake Pamvotis and the island where the monastery of Ayiou Nikolaou stands. From Ioannina the busiest route across northern Greece continues in the direction of Metsovo (capital of the "Vlachs," a minority of Romanian origin) and the Meteora. North of Ioannina is one of the most fascinating areas in Greece: it is advisable to take the road to Konitsa.

Forty kilometers north of the capital one enters the area of Zagorohoria, one of the best preserved corners of the country's mountain regions: thanks to an architectural reserve and rigorous conservation legislation, these clusters of villages with slate roofs and cobbled streets are still unspoiled. There are no eye-catching monuments in little places like Monodhendhri, Papingo and Vitsa, but interesting human settlements are to be found with one of the most fascinating European

74 top Situated right in the center of the Meteors, the village of Kastraki is a marvellous viewpoint over this incredible combination of nature and the work of man. It is also a meeting point for many of the mountaineers who wish to test their skill on the walls of the surroundings.

74-75 This photograph is proof of why the Meteors are called "the monasteries in the air." They were not built here just for defence; to the eyes of the monks, these majestic cliffs of soft rock must have seemed similar to the columns used by the stylites in the desert.

75 The Meteors rise at the edge of the Macedonian mountains at the beginning of the great Thessalonikan plain that stretches as far as the sea. From about 1000 AD until construction of the monasteries, the cliffs were a place of hermitage.

habitats as their backdrop. The Vikos gorge cuts through the limestone rock from Monodhendhri to the Papingo villages (Megalo and Mikro), its walls rising to heights of 400 meters. The gorge can be traversed on foot but hikers should be equipped with the right footwear and clothes. Papingo is the departure point for the excursion to Mount Gamila, a karst plateau of black and yellow rock reminiscent of a lunar landscape. Beyond Konitsa the road flanks Mount Grammos and the Albanian border before reaching the Macedonian town of Kastoria. An important center of Balkan Jews, who set up a flourishing leather industry here, Kastoria was built on the shores of the lake of the same name. Its architectural heritage includes numerous Byzantine churches, many dating back to the XI century, and handsome turreted mansions built for wealthy merchants between the 18th and early 20th centuries. Some 50 kilometers further north, on the once closely guarded border with Albania and the Republic of Macedonia, are the two Prespa lakes, separated by a causeway. The environment is interesting: it is possible to spend a few hours in the fishing village or in a bird sanctuary where as many as 177 species of birds can be spotted in the migration season. The best option at this point is to return to Kastoria: along the road to Konitsa, we turn off at Neapolis in the direction of Grevena, in the eastern part of the Pindhos range. From Grevena the Monasteries of the Meteora can be reached, one of the most famous sites of

the Greek Orthodox religion. These "monasteries in mid air" owe their existence to a dream of the young monk Athanasios who, over 600 years ago, felt the mystical call of these pinnacles of rock, situated at the edge of mountains that fringe the plain of Thessaly. From the 14th century onwards these spikes of friable rock with vertical walls attracted throngs of monks. During the decline of Byzantium, in particular, they offered effective places of refuge for Hellenism and Orthodoxy.

76 top The Byzantine fort of Platamonas in Macedonia overlooks a well-known seaside resort. Its distance from any other building emphasizes the military building. This is one of the best preserved remains of the empire of Constantinople.

76 bottom The ruins of the fort of Moglena in Macedonia are a vestige of the Byzantine period. Northern Greece has always been a frontier zone and suffered Slav invasions for centuries. To protect it, the emperor built a string of fortified castles in strategic locations.

120 kilometers of good roads, passing through Larissa then joining the coast-hugging highway to Salonika, separate the Meteora from a far more ancient place of worship, Mount Olympus. The dwelling-place of the deities of antiquity is permanently wrapped in cloud, and few of the thousands of hikers who complete the hard climb to its peak (Mitikas summit at 2917 meters above sea level) can honestly claim to have actually seen it. Even today Olympus – like every place sacred to man – preserves an undefinable atmosphere, already sensed at the foot of the path that ascends to the summit; it can be reached along a winding road that starts from the village of Litohoro, about 10 kilometers from the highway. Here the tiny monastery of Ayiou Ioannis – by the omnipresent spring – attracts tourists and locals from the scattered villages of Thessaly: reachable by car, it does not call for the climbing experience and gear essential for hikers who make the gruelling ascent to the refuge on Mitikas summit.

Olympus is an ideal point of departure for a tour of what were once the main centers of the Macedonian dynasty: at Dion (about 10 kilometers north of Litohoro, along the Athens-Salonika highway) Philip II maintained an important encampment and extensive ruins from the Hellenistic and Roman periods are still to be seen here; 40 kilometers further on is the site of the ancient city of Pydna where Olympias, mother of Alexander the Great, was killed. But the focal point of the Mace-donian itinerary is undoubtedly Philip II's tomb at Veryina. The spot can be reached by travelling 20 kilometers along the coast road and then heading inland for about the same distance in the direction of Veria. Conjecture that this might be the site of the lost city of Aegae, the very oldest capital of the Macedonian kingdom, was confirmed in 1977 with the discovery of the royal tombs. From a scenic standpoint the site has little to offer but the structure of this sumptuous burial place and its vivid colors are still clearly visible. Finds from the tombs (sarcophagus, diadem and royal scepter, as well as a gold shield and armor) are now exhibited at Salonika's archaeological museum. From Veryina our journey continues in the direction of Pella, capital of Macedonia during its most glorious period. On the way a stop can be made in Lefkadha (34 kilometers northwest of Veria, in the direction of Edessa, close to the village of Skidra), site of an impressive "Great Tomb" in orientalizing style, rarely visited nowadays. The remains of ancient Pella are about 40 kilometers east of Skidra, in the direction of Salonika. Evident among the ruins are traces of wide, right-angled roads and grand buildings: most prominent amongst them is the "palace" where three splendid mosaics dated to around 300 BC were unearthed. Depicting Dionysus riding a panther, a lion hunt and a fight between Amazons, they are now preserved in the local museum.

Salonika, the administrative center of northern Greece, is now barely 20 kilometers away. This city, much more than Athens, is emblematic of the colorful, cosmopolitan spirit typical of the Balkans before the great ethnic purges of the 20th century. Something of this spirit survives in the old Turkish quarter, perched on the age-old hillside acropolis. Tucked inside city walls of Hellenistic origin is a labyrinth of tiny streets lined with characteristic timber-built houses, most of them – until recently – in a fairly delapidated condition. Now, as in older parts of Athens, rather better-heeled occupants are moving in, more for the area's snob value than out of any real need.

In the lower part of the city, evidence of the Greek and Byzantine urban layout emerges here and there from the fabric of modern developments. All things told, thanks to planning schemes that have given breathing space to the historic buildings and monuments of the city center, Salonika is a more pleasant and liveable place than Greece's chaotic capital.

Symbolically the city is a crossroads: it was a major center on the Via Egnatia, the busy Roman-Byzantine artery that linked Italy and Constantinople; today it is also the second port of Greece – guarded by the Turkish White Tower – where ships are loaded with Macedonia's renowned tobacco, exported worldwide. The Roman road still crosses the city today: beside it is the Arch of Galerius, with only

two of its original four pillars surviving. North of the Via Egnatia, close to one another in the very heart of the city, are the Turkish Bath, the church of Panaghia Chalkeon, oldest of the Byzantine basilicas, and the Hellenistic-Roman agora. Also not far from the Roman road are the churches of Ayia Sofia, dating from the Iconoclast period, and Ayios Yioryios, the rotunda originally designed as a mausoleum for Emperor Galerius; it was converted into a church at the end of the 4th century AD and became the city's most distinctive monument. Completing the architectural heritage of this wealthy Byzantine center are a series of monuments in the Turkish upper citadel: the domed church of Hosios David, the Vlatadhon monastery and the churches of Ayios Nikolaos and the Taxiarchs.

But in the first few decades of the 20th century "beautiful Thessaloniki" was deprived of the atmosphere that labelled it a real city of the Levant: first its Turkish community disappeared, then – during World War II – came the elimination of its Jewish population, a lively minority actively involved in trade throughout the Mediterranean and especially with similar Jewish communities in Spain and Egypt. By some cruel quirk of fate cosmopolitan Salonika was also the birthplace of Mustafa Kemal who eventually became known as Ataturk and played a leading role in the division of these territories.

79 left The photograph shows what is known as "Aristotle's beach," one of the Greeks' own favorite tourist destinations. Located on the Cassandra peninsula the west "finger" of Khalkidhiki, it is not far from Salonika.

79 right The statue by Harpocrates depicting Dionysus as a child is one of the works of art in Salonika's archaeological museum where one of the largest collections of archaeological finds from the Macedonian tombs of Pella and Vergina is to be found.

80 top left One
mostly travels on
foot in the
theocratic republic
of Mount Athos.
The monasteries are
generally about one
hour's hike from one
another. The monks
are divided into
different categories;

an elected
government and a
form of justice
administration
exist. At a
superficial level, it
appears that life in
this special republic
continues much as it
did two hundred
years ago.

80 center left The
kitchens in one of the
monasteries of the
Holy Mount is in
continuous use and
not only for the
benefit of the monks.
All monasteries offer
guest quarters to
welcome pilgrims
and tourists. The only
condition, of course,
is that they are male
and adult.

80 bottom left The
monasteries of Mount
Athos do not contain
especially old works of
art. Most of the
frescoes were painted
between the 17th and
the 19th centuries.
Two schools of art were
responsible for the
paintings, the first
was from Macedonia,
the second from Crete.

East of Salonika, in the Chalcidian peninsula, are beach resorts thronging with Greek and international tourists and a "monastic oasis" on the Mount Athos peninsula. The largest community of its kind in Europe, it is separated from the modern world by a boundary beyond which no females may set foot. The monks' theocratic republic which has long been the spiritual heart of the Orthodox religion is located in a part of Greece now totally committed to the world of computers and the Internet. For those who may cross the boundary, Athos has some amazing sights to reveal, not least of which is the scenery unrivalled in the Mediterranean for its preserved beauty.

80 right A large
religious festival takes
place at the
monastery of Iviron,
where the monk
Gabriel performed his
amazing walk on the
water. The monk had

found the icon of the
Portaitissa Virgin –
still held at Iviron –
in the midst of the
waves. The miracle is
attributed to the
painting, today half-
erased.

80-81 The monk Athanasious founded the monastery of Aghia Lavra in 963 which was followed by the many others on the peninsula of Mount Athos. The monastic community reached its peak in 1400 but after the spread of the Ottoman empire, it created a close diplomatic relationship with the sultan.

81 top The monastery dedicated to Simon Peter stands atop the promontory facing onto the west coast of the holy peninsula. As in other monastic complexes on Mount Athos, the rule followed here by the monks is marked by their life together.

82 top The
easternmost city in
Greece is Kavalla,
one of Macedonia's
principal centers.
The lovely Moslem
quarter that dates
from the 18th
century was built
around the
monastery of
Mehmet Ali, the
sultan of Egypt.

82-83 The scene of the
battle between Brutus
and Cassius on one
side and Octavius
and Anthony or the
other, Philippi can
boast Roman and
Byzantine remains.
The city gained its
importance from
being one of the stops
on the Via Egnatia,
the Roman road that
led eastwards. The
photograph shows the
ruins of an early
Christian church.

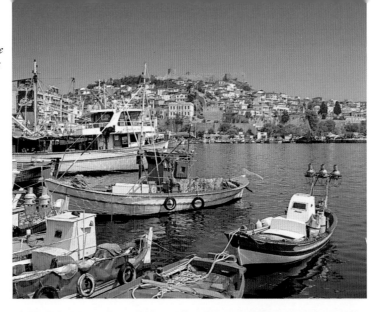

Extending from the promontory of Haghion Horos, the holy mountain of Athos, to the border with Turkey is the fertile Thrace territory. It is, alongside with Macedonia, the most important agricultural area of Greece with its production of tobacco and rice. Two cities of interest are Kavala, with its large Muslim quarter, and nearby Philippi, site of mortal combat between the two factions of Julius Caesar's successors.

On the marshy coastal plain are Xanthi and Komotini, then Alexandhroupoli, populated mainly by refugees once part of the huge Hellenic diaspora, along the coasts of the Black Sea and the Asian Aegean.

At the very edge of the Greek territory is the splendid Evros Delta, one of the most important wetlands in the eastern Mediterranean, and a temporary and tranquil home to countless migrating birds.

83 top The growth of Kavalla in Macedonia has surrounded the fort. Despite the rapid urbanization of recent times, the ancient castle that was built to control the important Roman road for communications with the east and the surrounding sea can still be made out.

83 bottom The ruins of the temple of Poseidon can be visited on the site of Aliki on the island of Thassos close to the Thracian coast. Active from the 7th century BC until Roman times, the sanctuary stood on a narrow strip of land surrounded by thick pine woods. On the island there are also two Byzantine churches.

THE PELOPONNESE
THE "ISLAND" OF PELOPS

84 top left The modern port of Patras at the mouth of the Gulf of Patras is one of the most common means of arriving in Greece. It is mostly visitors heading for Athens and then on to the many islands who make use of the comfortable and best equipped Greek port.

84 top right The house of the priests of Mycenae stands at the lowest part of the acropolis. Various layers of remains of the different epochs since first occupation of the site can be seen on the hill. Earliest inhabitation was from 3000 BC, before the Achaeans arrived in the peninsula.

84-85 Wild and baked by the sun, the island of Elafonisos near the eastern tip of the Peloponnese looks like a fragment of desert flung into the sea.

85 The cargo being carried through the Corinthian canal almost seems to skim the walls. The isthmus that connects the Peloponnese to mainland Greece was dug at the end of the 19th century but the idea was much older: the first to attempt the task was the Roman emperor Caligula.

The name Peloponnese means literally "island of Pelops" (whose father, Tantalus, was punished with eternal hunger and thirst for having revealed to mankind the secrets of the gods). It is the land where the bellicose Sparta and cities like Mycenae, Argos, Corinth and Olympia once prospered. With respect to the Athens of antiquity, it represents another face of classical Greece. Technically an island since 1893 when the completion of the Corinth Canal separated it from the mainland, the Peloponnese is a geographical and historical mosaic, made up of landscapes sometimes seemingly borrowed from mainland Greece or other parts of the Mediterranean. The countryside in Nemea is reminiscent of Tuscany, Epidaurus has features typical of Attica while Arcadia – a wilder region than its name suggests – resembles the mountains of Epirus and Thessaly. Other places belong instead to a world apart: Mycenae, first and foremost, but also the Byzantine cities of Mystra and Monemvassia, and the beautiful Mani peninsula, southernmost point of the Peloponnese.

Patras, overlooking the gulf of the same name, is the capital of the Peloponnese and the region's most modern and sprawling city. It is the gateway to Italy and the rest of Europe, busy in summer with the comings and goings of tourists. A highway heads towards Athens along the coast of the Gulf of Corinth. Little more than 60 kilometers from Patras is Dhiakofto, starting point of the most spectacular railway line in the country: its tiny train clambers up the mountains along the narrow Vouraikos gorge. Passengers pile out at the one stop along the line, by a café in Zahlorou. From here they walk to the monastery of Mega Spilio and the large cave nearby where – according to legend – the Virgin Mary appeared to a humble shepherd. Back on the old train, its final destination is Kalavrita, another place hard hit by the horrors of war: here a memorial stone commemorates one thousand local men shot dead by occupying German troops in a brutal reprisal. It was from the monastery of Ayia Lavra, higher up the mountain, that in 1821 the archbishop of Patras gave the signal for the rising against the Ottoman empire. Kalavrita lies in a valley at the heart of the Peloponnese mountains, where the Panakaic, Helmos and Erimanthos ranges converge.

86 top This view of
the fortified walls
snaking around the
top of the Acropolis is
one of the loveliest to
be seen in ancient
Corinth.

86 bottom The temple
of Apollo is
undoubtedly the most
spectacular
monument in ancient
Corinth. The building
is one of the oldest
remains of classical
Greek culture. It was
built between 550 and
525 BC on the site of
an older shrine.

Back on the coast, and 70 kilometers further along the highway, we come to Corinth. The modern city has developed not far from the canal dug in the 19th century to shorten the maritime route between the Ionian and Aegean seas. Before its completion ships were forced to circumnavigate the Peloponnese and round the perilous Cape Matapan. In ancient times vessels were instead carried overland, pulled on an ingenious wheeled platform across the narrow strip of land where water now flows; transporting these boats was a major source of revenues to fill the coffers of ancient Corinth. Situated in an enviably strategic position, the city was able to keep watch over the two seas and guard the only access via land to the Peloponnese. According to contemporary writers, Corinth enjoyed the most licentious lifestyle and culture of

the ancient world: a thousand sacred prostitutes practised their own particular form of devotion in the temple of Astarte, the eastern goddess of love. It was here that St. Paul carried out his apostolic mission: in his *Letters to the Corinthians* he urged the people of the city to repent and seek salvation, abandoning their entrenched self-indulgent and unvirtuous ways. Acrocorinth is situated in a splendid position, looking out towards the sea. Successive waves of occupants – Greeks, Romans, Venetians, Frankish Crusaders, Turks – contributed to the buildings of the acropolis; the walls and the fortress are still standing. From this vantage point, rather than from the ruins of the Roman agora, it is easy to understand just how much power and prosperity the ancient city acquired from its ability to keep watch on two seas, then far apart. Extending beneath Corinth is the Argolid, in terms of history and archaeology one of the richest regions of Greece. Continuing from Corinth along the Aegean coast we reach Epidaurus, site of the most famous sanctuary dedicated to Asclepius, the god of healing: around the ruined temple it is still possible to identify the remains of "dormitories" where patients slept to await a visitation from the god. The Romans added spa baths to the complex, but the most stunning sight at Epidaurus is the ancient theater, with 14,000 seats the largest and best conserved in the whole of Greece. And at the summer Festival of Classical Drama good use is still made of its outstanding attributes, including excellent acoustics.

86-87 The Byzantine, Frank and Venetian walls form the enormous fortification of Acrocorinth. Whoever controlled the citadel was able to dominate the passage between the Aegean and Ionian seas both militarily and economically.

87 top left The theater of Sikiona stands on a slight slope dotted with oak trees in front of an agricultural plain. The theater is not on the mass tourist trail but is known and appreciated by connoisseurs of Grecia Minor.

87 top right The theater in Epidaurus is the best-preserved of Greek classical theaters. Its existence was closely linked to that of the sanctuary of the Greek god of medicine, Asclepius. The performances in the theater had both liturgical and therapeutic functions.

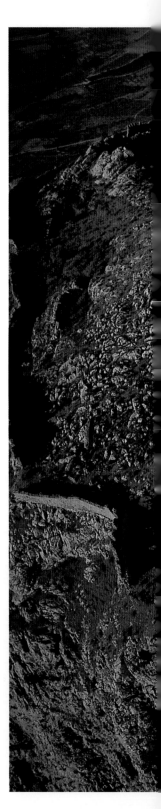

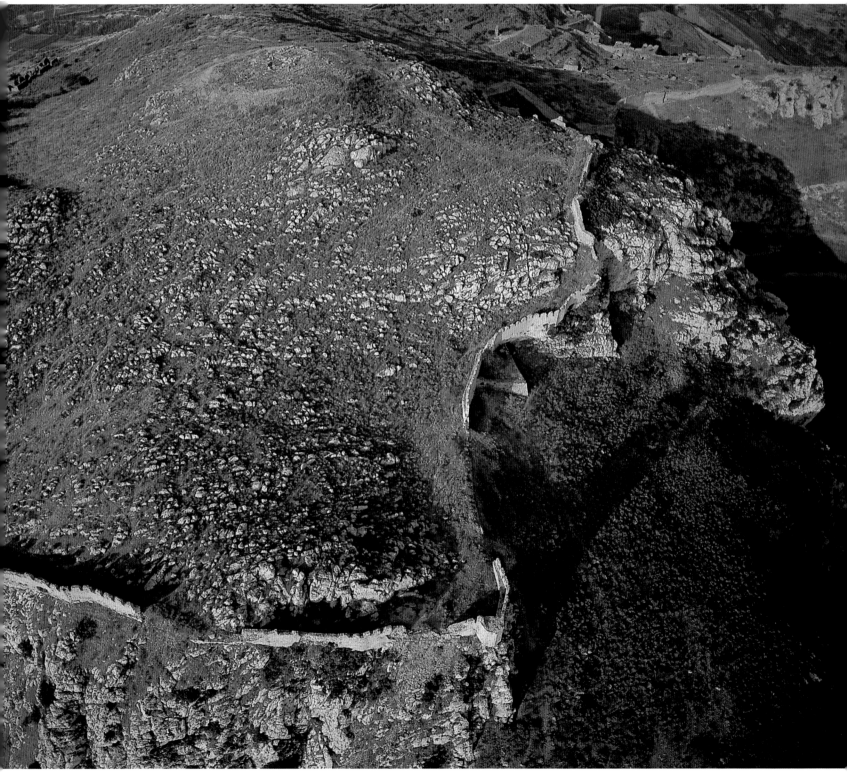

87

Nafplio (also written as Nauplia or Navplion), 50 kilometers from Epidaurus, is situated on the most "inland" shores of the Gulf of the Argolid. This medieval city, dominated by a handsome Venetian fort, was the capital of the first Greek kingdom. The parliament of "micro-Greece" (not much larger than the Peloponnese) met in the old disused mosque, while the royal residence was the fortified Venetian citadel, now housing the Nafplia Palace, belonging to the National Tourist Board.

88 top The spur of rock that stands over Navplion seems like the prow of a ship in the middle of the Aegean. The spur allowed the large fortification to be built in what the Venetians had called "the Naples of the Romans."

88 center The aerial view shows the walls of the medieval castle in Argos to good effect. Particularly famous for its Mycenaean acropolis, the town that gave its name to the region of Argolis was an important link in the string of fortifications used by the Ottoman empire.

88 bottom The Turkish tower of Bourzi stands at the tip of the promontory of Methoni in the south of the Peloponnese. It is part of the large fortress designed by the Venetians and later strengthened by the Ottomans. It is still in excellent condition.

88-89 The aerial photograph shows the layout of the ancient defences of Navplion, the first capital of Greece which, after independence from the Ottoman empire, corresponded to the Peloponnese. The city lies on the Argolis Gulf at the feet of an imposing Venetian citadel.

90 top left The tiny port of Aghio Kiprianos is just one of the many little known ports and beaches on the Mani peninsula, the middle "finger" of the Peloponnese. Whoever controlled the Morea (this was the medieval and Venetian name for the peninsula) had to deal with the troublesome Maniots, the descendants of the Spartans.

90 top right Pilos bay is one of the most beautiful in Greece. It is also known as the Gulf of Navarino from the name of the Slav peoples (Avars) that settled there. The bay was the scene of the victory of the allied French, English and Russian fleets against the Turkish and Egyptian fleets during the war of Greek independence.

90-91 The port of Ghithio lies at the entrance to the Mani peninsula, one of the three tips of the Peloponnese. Ghithio is a pleasant stop-off on the way south and is a well-known fishing port.

Heading inland and northwards, we reach the most important and amazing archaeological site of the Argolid: the ruins of the prehistoric citadel of Mycenae. The legendary city of Agamemnon is set on a hill against a backdrop of high mountains, and encircled by grey stone cyclopean walls. The acropolis is entered through the celebrated Lion Gate, surmounted by the stylized forms of two lions, now headless. Inside the double ring of walls are a first circle of graves and the remains of imposing buildings dated to 1500 BC; the ruins occupying the upper part of the site have been identified by archaeologists as those of Mycenae's royal palace. Outside the circuit of walls, not far from the citadel, narrow passageways lead into the huge mounds that conceal the tombs of the House of Atreus. The archaeological treasures of Mycenae, which were unearthed by the pragmatic dreamer Schliemann, are undoubtedly among the most fascinating ever discovered. And an evocative setting for the cyclopean walls and tholos tombs is provided by barren rocky slopes and ravines, yellow grass withered by the burning sun and the almost deafening chirping of crickets.

Less stunning, though coeval and similar in layout, are the remains of nearby Argos and Tyrins, between Mycenae and Nafplio. Another style and a more Classical atmosphere pervade the ruins of Nemea, sited in a verdant landscape dotted with cypresses. Descending the coast, the scenery be-comes more rugged. At Leonidhi, beneath the towering bulk of Mount Parnon, the road turns inland; from this point onwards high cliffs edge the shoreline, accessible only by boat or with the ferry from Pireas that calls at the village of Kiparissi. Just south of this deserted stretch of coast is Monemvassia. The spendid medieval seaport clings to a tiny island, once linked to the mainland by a causeway. Its fortified center, encircled by walls, was possessed through the centuries by Byzantines, Venetians and Turks. For the kingdom of the Morea (as the Peloponnese was called in medieval times) Monemvassia was a stronghold of immense importance during the wars not infrequently waged in the region. And it is still a spectacular town today, with a mix of styles known to the experts as Italo-Byzantine.

After Monemvassia fell into Byzantine hands, the Frankish princes founded Mystra, some 100 kilometers away. It overlooks the valley of Lakonia, not far from the ancient site of Sparta. The ruined remains of the city spill down the slopes of Taiyettos, one of the loveliest mountains in Greece, as far as the fortified walls. Preserved inside the wall circuit are monasteries and frescoed churches; the upper town is dominated by the castle.

94 center The church of Aghia Sophia in Mistras is almost intact. The city passed from the Franks to the Byzantine empire shortly after it was founded. The

Byzantines made it into one of its most important fortresses. It was abandoned after the bloody repression of the revolt against the Turks at the end of the 18th century.

94 bottom The monastery of Perivletos, the dome of which is shown in the photograph, is famous for the elegance of its murals.

94-95 Apart from Monemvassìa, the other large Byzantine center in medieval Morea was Mistras. Built upon a conical rock not far from ancient Sparta, the citadel still preserves its original character in its many religious buildings.

96 top left Little remains of Athens' proud rival. Sparta was a city without superb monuments, almost as a reaction against the grandeur and artistic liberality of the "soft" capital of Attica. Therefore, the quality of Sparta's ruins are not so impressive.

96 top right The tradition of towers belonging to family clans is still prevalent in Kotronas in the region of Mani. Normally the entrance is on the first floor rather than on the ground. A ladder up to it can be pulled up in case of need which helps to prevent not only invaders but intruders.

96-97 The village of Vathia is a good place to see typical Maniot towers-cum-houses. Unlike the rest of Greece, the people of the central peninsula at the southern tip of the Peloponnese are very reserved.

97 top Openness and peace are the characteristics of the archaeological site of Olympia. The city of games and sacred truces still stimulates a sense of tranquillity and relaxation in visitors. The ancients usually thought that these feelings were inspired by a spiritus loci, a sort of divinity associated with the place.

97 center This is another classical theater near the sacred city of Olympia. This is Mantinea in the center of eastern Arcadia.

Next to nothing remains of Sparta, first destroyed by Alaric and subsequently invaded by wave after wave of Slavs. The descendants of the Dorians eventually abandoned the city and sought refuge in the Mani, medieval Magna.

The "middle finger" of the three peninsulas at the foot of the Peloponnese, this tongue of land begins about 50 kilometers south of Sparta.

Still visible in the region are traces of a society very different to the prevailing culture of Greece.

The villages of the Mani were once populated by feudal clans, who lived in tower houses with loophole windows and doors set high in their walls, entered solely by using wooden ladders.

In the past this corner of the Peloponnese remained detached from mainstream Greek culture: a noticeable and eloquent example of its difference is the absence of village squares, traditional meeting-places of Greek communities.

In the almost abandoned villages, the people do not like to mix with strangers: it is natural that this particularity recalls something of the harsh character of ancient Spartan aristocracy.

An annual event in one village of the Mani is the gathering of a clan that claims to originate not from neighboring Sparta but from a cadet branch of the Medici family, in Renaissance Florence, this pro- viding testimony of of the prosperous trade links of the past.

Heading northeast, to complete our tour of the Peloponnese, we come to Kalamata, famous for olives exported all over the world, and – approaching the Ionian coast – the archaeological sites of Messene, Pylos and Vasses.

Tucked in a valley amid gently rolling hills, the archaeological site of Olympia has an evocative atmosphere that sets it apart from the "wilder" Archaic cities. For this place was the foremost religious center of the Greek world, a symbol of ethnic, linguistic and spiritual identity.

At four-yearly intervals the imposing sanctuary dedicated to Zeus provided the venue for the Panhellenic games, at which the Greeks laid down their arms during a sacred truce recognized by all the city-states.

Excavations were started on the site by the French towards the end of the 1700s, and subsequently continued by the Germans. Among the ruins unearthed are the gymnasium, baths, pools, athlete's living quarters, stadium and hippodrome of the first city to have hosted the Olympics. In this capital of sport the city-states of Greece continued to compete amicably in trials of strength and skill until the 4th century AD, when Theodosius ruled that the games be abolished.

97 bottom The surroundings of Olympia are filled with small and little known archaeological sites. One example is the lovely ancient theater of Megalopolis, located in the heart of Arcadia. The building, dating back to the 4th century BC, was the largest of Greece as it could seat 21,000 spectators on its ten tiers.

THE ISLANDS, GREECE'S WHITE AND BLUE CROWNING GLORY

THE IONIAN ISLANDS

98 Zante, or Zákinthos, can boast proper cliffs. This green island also has splendid beaches. It is said that on Laganas beach is the finest sand in Greece.

98-99 A beach in Kalati on Kithira, the southernmost of the Ionian islands, was the legendary birth-place of Aphrodite.

99 top left The small town of Zákinthos was destroyed by an earthquake in 1953. The Venetian remains are thus limited to the fortified citadel that overlooks the capital.

99 top right Leukas, or Lefkàs, was the island of Santa Maura to the Venetians. The photograph shows the village of Nidri on one side of the romantic bay. The island is almost attached to the mainland by a strip of land.

Geographical statistics put the number of Greek islands at 2,000 but discounting the small ones – sometimes little more than large rocks – 200 or so is a more realistic figure. Not only are they natural assets of importance to the world at large; they are also, and especially, a gradually disappearing legacy of heterogeneous cultures. None but the largest islands have a working population during the winter months: today only tourism brings people to the Greek islands. Until around 1920 these places were still inhabited year round and were busy with fishing and sponge-diving, not just seasonal activities. Diminished economic importance and depopulation are particularly evident in archipelagoes like the Dodecanese, once among the country's most prosperous regions, mainly on account of its closeness to the shores of Asia.

This general trend has had its ups and downs. For example, the discovery of oil in the Aegean recently led to a dispute between the Greek and Turkish governments, both anxious to exploit any prospective oilfields. The Greeks' eastern neighbors claim they are entitled to any natural resources found within the area of the "continental plateau" while the Greeks naturally have no intention of giving up any rights of their own. In actual fact the whole controversy died a natural death: tourism and oil wells hardly can co-exist, above and beyond the serious risks posed for the environ-

ment at large.

An exception to this tendency to progressive abandonment is fortunately offered by the Ionian Islands, strung out along the westernmost shores of Greece. Like stepping stones across a stream, the Ionian islands form a bridge between Greece and the rest of Europe, from an historical as well as geographical standpoint. A Venetian possession until 1797, they were then occupied by the French and for a while became a Turco-Russian protectorate. The French returned in 1807, to be replaced, after the fall of Napoleon, by the British. Then, towards the end of the 19th century, they formed the Heptanesos (seven islands) Republic which they remained until eventually ceded to the kingdom of Greece. The town of Corfu, capital of the Ionian, bears evidence of centuries of outside influence: the traditional dress worn by the women closely resembles the costumes of Italy, the esplanade used for military exercises is a typically French legacy, the structure of the Venetian citadel was extensively modified by the British. Located north of the Corfiote capital and open to visitors is the Achilleion, a palace once owned by the beautiful and famous Elizabeth, Empress of Austria, who prided herself on being a benefactress of the arts. Today, with the tourist industry contributing to the transformation of local roadways and mentality, Corfu is still the most international of the islands.

100 top Paxos is a port for sailboats and yachts. There are two villages, Gaios (in the photograph) and Lakka which lies further north. Both were built facing the continental coast.

100-101 The beach at Antisamos on Cephalonia, the largest of the Ionian islands and the one with the greatest variety of landscapes. The island's name is derived from kefali which means head, but which by extension also means mountain.

A delightfully Greek atmosphere instead greets visitors to Paxos and Antipaxos, twin islands opposite the Epirot coast, and Lefkas, separated from the mainland by a channel hardly wider than a ship's bridge. Ithaca may be set in a "wine-colored sea," as lyrically defined by Homer, but travellers hoping to recognize places described in the Odyssey may be in for some disappointment.

The archaeological sites are barely visible and ongoing excavations are often closed to the public. But the Arethousa spring and the Grotto of the Nymphs are more than adequate consolation for anyone who comes here looking for evidence of a world that disappeared almost three thousand years ago.

Continuing southwards, Cephalonia appears on the horizon. This island of the "Head" or of the "Mountain," suffered severe damage in the 1953 earthquake and its two main towns, Sami and Argostoli, are now thoroughly modern. But the island's old charm survives intact in the villages of Assos, with its Venetian fortress, and Fiskardho where old Italian houses overlook the harbor. A short way along the coast is Markopoulo where every year, shortly before the Assumption of the Virgin festival in August, large numbers of snakes suddenly appear; the phenomenon is by tradition considered part natural, part magic.

101 top Andipaxoi is rarely visited by the majority of international tourists although it is close to Corfu. It is preferred by lovers of untamed nature.

101 bottom Mirtos beach is justly one of the most famous on Cephalonia. The white sand and the lovely turquoise of the sea are the main attractions for both local and foreign tourists.

Italian and Greek reminiscences about their respective "Risorgimento" on the island of Zante (or Zákinthos) is found only in the works of Italian poet Ugo Foscolo and in the patriotic odes of Dionissios Solomos, author of the Greek national anthem. Here in the "flower of the Levant" (as the Venetians called Zante), most of the old constructions were completely destroyed by the same catastrophic earthquake that hit Cephalonia. Lastly, at the very foot of the Peloponese is Kithira, also belonging to the Ionian islands.

THE CYCLADES

104 top Delos is the center of the circle of the Cyclades islands both historically and geographically. The name of the archipelago is representative (kiklos means circle). The photograph shows the theater set against the backdrop of the port.

104 center Apollo is supposed to have been born at Delos and it is to him that the sacred city is dedicated. For the ancients, Delos was not a true island but a ship anchored in the heart of the Aegean. For many decades it was forbidden to give birth or to die here as Delos was purified land.

The Cyclades archipelago best fits the image foreigners most often have of Greece. And not only on account of fabled islands like Mikonos, with its inviting beaches, picturesque windmills and hundreds of discotheques in which to dance the night away... Their attraction lies essentially in the combined appeal of fascinating vestiges of antiquity, like the sacred island of Delos, dedicated to Apollo, and the sun-baked scenery of the southern Mediterranean.

The archipelago got its name from the arrangement of the islands in a circle (*kyklos*) around Delos, sacred to the sun, for over a thousand years the religious and political center of the Aegean Sea. Its monuments are among the best preserved in all Greece: the Sacred Way leads to the ruins of the Sanctuaries of Apollo and Artemis and to the Ancient Lake on which swans and geese sacred to the sun-god once swam. With no accommodation available on Delos, sightseers must make their base on nearby Mikonos or Tinos, famous for celebrations marking the Feast of the Assumption of the Virgin (August 15). About 100 kilometers from Delos and Mikonos is Naxos, still a haven for anyone fleeing islands blighted by package-tour atmosphere and packed private beaches.

104 bottom The colossal statue in the marble quarry at Apollona on the north coast of Naxos has just been rough cast. Its disquieting profile might suggest a resemblance with the statues on Easter Island.

104-105 The gate of the archaic temple of Apollo dominates the capital of Naxos, the largest of the Cyclades islands. According to legend, Theseus left Arianna here on his return from Crete; Arianna had helped Theseus in his task of defeating the Minotaur.

105 top The stone lions on the terrace of the same name are the easily recognized symbol of Delos, perhaps the best preserved of Greece's archaeological cities. Undoubtedly, the island-cum-sanctuary is one of the country's loveliest places.

Santorini, southernmost of the Cyclades, is currently the most popular destination for summer visitors. And there is much to attract them: their first glimpse of its red and yellow volcanic soil, the huge and spectacular crater invaded by the sea after an eruption in protohistoric times, exceptionally beautiful scenery. The ruins of Thira date to the Dorian period, while archaeologists excavating at Akrotiri have identified the remains of a Minoan city, buried by the tremendous eruption that around 1450 BC caused the west side of the island to sink beneath the sea. Splendid frescoes of dancers and dolphins unearthed in the royal palace are now exhibited in the National Museum in Athens. The antiquity of this site has led a few scientists with fervid imaginations to identify Santorini with the legendary Atlantis.

106 top The ancient village of Pyrgos stands on red and yellow volcanic hills. The name Santorini is a distorsion of Santa Irene, the Venetian name for the island, also known as "the very beautiful."

106 bottom The discovery of ancient Thera from the Minoan era launched Santorini into the world of tourism. Until some years ago, the capital could only be reached from the port on horseback.

106-107 On Santorini, the southernmost of the Cyclades, it is easy to understand why the Greek flag is white and blue.

107 top Thera, the capital of Santorini, stands on the edge of an ancient volcanic crater and only a small island is left: many believe that the explosion that destroyed the island gave rise to the myth of Atlantis.

107 bottom The volcano is responsible for the attraction of Thera, which overlooks one of the bluest seas in the world from 100 meters of height.

108-109 On account of Santorini's natural conformation Thira, the capital, developed like the immense cavea of an amphitheater, overlooking the Mediterranean and facing west.

110 The restoration of the royal palace of Knossos has inevitably roused the dissent of archaeological purists. The reconstruction cannot be called scientific but strikes a chord with the tourists. The picture shows the entrance.

111 top left Archaeologists also made a heavy-handed "interpretative" effort at restoring the frescoes of bearers of food and drinks but the grace of the originals is still evident beneath the restoration.

111 top right The Minoan kings received the homage of their subjects in the throne room from 1700 BC but also decided here on commercial relations with the other economic centers of the area: continental Greece, the Cyclades and Egypt.

111 center right More than 800 rooms in the palace of Knossos still remain, but it is probable that there were originally over 1300 connected via corridors. That is enough to justify the legend of the "labyrinth" in which King Minos made his son, the Minotaur, live. The picture shows the shield room.

Lastly, in the far south lies Crete. The history of the Mediterranean's third-largest island has close ties with mainland Greece, but the two have not always advanced in perfect unison. An apt example is offered by the tale of King Minos, who exacted from Athens an annual tribute of 14 youths, to be offered as a sacrifice to the Minotaur, mythical half-man, half-beast eventually slaughtered by Theseus. At that time the Minoans with their advanced culture were in direct conflict with the towns – then little more than herders' settlements – scattered over the Greek peninsula. The sumptuous palaces of Cnossus, Festos and Malia built in Crete over four thousand years ago attest to the wealth of the Minoan civilization, crushed 500 years later by Achaean invaders. Things subsequently remained dormant for many centuries. The fortunes of Crete revived only in the 13th century AD when, after Arab and Byzantine domination, the island contended by Genoese and Venetians came under the control of the Serenissima Republic. For the next 400 years the island flourished again. Its art, in particular, was much bolder than that of mainland Greece, as is clearly evident in the naturalism of a Cretan who became famous in Spain: Domenikos Theotokopoulos, known as El Greco. The twenty-year seige of Candia ended with Crete's return to the Ottoman empire in 1669. Little was heard of the island again, outside its own immediate sphere, until World War II, when the occupation armies were engaged in fierce battles there for many months. The culture of Crete has long exalted courage and throughout Greece its people are reputed to be plucky and determined; still today, in the *kafenion* of the island, it is not unusual to see old men wearing black hairnets and with handlebar moustaches, standing erect and proud like warriors of old.

The amazing civilization that developed on Crete is known to the whole world from the ruined palaces of Cnossus and Festos, built between 1900 and 1700 BC and destroyed by the same natural disaster that razed Santorini to the ground around 1400 BC. The remains of Cnossus, located just a few kilometers from Iraklion, the island's capital, have been restored in a perhaps fanciful but nonetheless effective way. They consist essentially of the luxurious palace, said – of course – to have been the home of King Minos, where long, winding corridors are reminiscent of the legendary labyrinth. It was certainly an imposing structure, occupying an area of over 20,000 sqare meters, with walls entirely painted and frescoed. The palace of Festos, standing on a well-fortified acropolis in the southern part of the island, is decidedly less opulent. Many pieces found at Cnossus, Festos and other archaeological sites in Crete (Gortys, Malia, Tilissos, Lissos) are conserved in the museum at Iraklion, the world's best endowed showcase of Minoan art and artefacts.

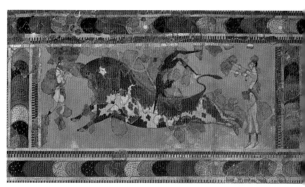

111 bottom right One of the most famous frescoes at Knossos is that of the Taurocatapsia, the celebration of a rite that bears some similarities to bull-fighting though less cruel to the bull. Young acrobats somersault onto the back of the animal in an exhibition of exceptional courage.

Crete's southern shores offer some unexpected bonuses, above and beyond its splendid sea. Midway along the coast is the typical seaside town of Matala, with tiny white houses creeping down to the beach. Continuing westwards the road abandons the coast, here swampy in places, and winds further and further into the barren Cretan mountains before eventually descending towards Selia.

Some 30 kilometers further on is Frangokastello, a handsome medieval fort rising out of a coastal plain. From Sfakion – the region's capital, about 10 kilometers west – it is possible to take a closer look at this lovely stretch of coast from a characteristic *kaikia*; from the harbor small ferries also provide a shuttle service to Ayia Roumeli, at the mouth of the famous Samarian

112 top On a flat hill not far from the southern sea stand the large ruins of the royal palace of Festos *on which Italian archaeologists have long worked. Unlike Knossos, Festos has not been rebuilt .* *112 center Crete is the island where the Venetians and Turks fought. It is dotted with forts such as that of Spinalonga, shown in the image.* *112 bottom The lion of St. Mark still prowls on the fort of Heraklion. The Venetian republic dominated the island for about 450 years.*

gorge, one of the places in Greece that attracts most visitors.

Created by the erosive action of atmospheric agents, it is certainly beautiful.

Starting inland from the village of Omalos, high on a plateau, it is possible to traverse the entire gorge in a day, walking between the towering walls of limestone rock right down to the sea.

Not far distant, among the rugged *Lefka Ori* (White Mountains), a natural wilderness is home to the last remaining *kri-kri*, a goat that lives only in this remote corner of the planet.

112-113 The beach at Khora Sfakion, on the south coast of Crete, faces onto the limpid waters of the Libyan sea.

113 top The Djamissi, the "small mosque," stands out in the middle of the port of Khaniá, Crete's second largest town.

113 center The Venetian fort overlooks the entrance to the port of Heraklion, the ancient city of Candia. The city resisted the Ottoman siege for 23 years.

113 bottom In the port of Rethimno in the north of Crete, many "caïques," the traditional Greek fishing boat, can still be found.

114 top In the interior of Greece's largest island, nature soon takes the upper hand over the works of man. Proceeding from the bay of Stomio towards the offshots of the Lefka Ori on the west coast, one can still see the sea from this complex of holy buildings.

114 bottom The Levka Ori (White Mountains) run down the center of the island. Little known and even less visited, they reach 2,400 meters in height. Only the Gorge of Samarià is known to the public at large.

115-118 Small islands, lagoons, white sand and a landscape that reminds some of Palestine: Cretan beaches, particularly those less well-known such as the bay of Balos at Gramvusa, have surprises in store even for the most demanding visitors.

119 The beaches along the island's southern shores, overlooking the Libyan Sea, are the most stunning of all. The tourist structures are recent additions: until some years ago getting here was far from easy. The photo shows a stretch of the coast near Loutro.

120 top The photograph shows Poros in the gulf of Vagonia. The island lies close to the Pelopponese coast which its environment closely resembles.

120-121 Baked by the sun, Hydra contends with the other islands in the Saronic Gulf to be the best-loved by Atheneans. It is gaunt and wild like the not too distant Cyclades.

Travelling northwards along the east coast of the Pelopponese, we reach the Saronic Gulf, opposite Athens: the islands rising out of these tranquil waters are the closest to the capital and therefore a popular choice for weekending tourists. Gracing Aegina is the Temple of Aphaia, one of the loveliest monuments of the classical period; in winter a colorful note is added to the scene by *kaikia*, the island's traditional boats, decorated for the Christmas festivities with oranges and jasmine. The rugged islands of Poros, Hydra and Spetses (safe havens for Christians in the days of the Ottoman rule) really come to life only during the tourist season.

121 top The stretch of water between Poros and the Peloponnese is very narrow. It seems that Argolide is almost within a stone throw.

*121 center
The temple of Aphea at Aegina is certainly one of the loveliest examples of*

Doric art. Aphea was a local goddess whose origin was much older than those members of the classical Greek pantheon.

121 bottom Hydra is a popular tourist port and an inevitable stop for those who island-hop along the Greek coast.

*122 top The white
houses in the village
of Skiros cascade
down a hill in sight
of the sea. The village
is famous for local
crafts such as wooden
carving and fine
embroidery.*

*122-123 The green
woods are a rest for
the eyes on Skiros, the
greenest island in the
Sporades. According
to legend, it was the
Skiriots that killed
the Athenean hero,
Theseus whose bones
have long been
contended between
the Skiriots and the
hero's compatriots.*

EUBOEA, THE SPORADES, AND THE ASIATIC ISLANDS

123 top Skiathos in the northern Sporades is famous for its marvelous beaches (Lalaria beach is seen in the picture).

123 center Euboea is the second largest Greek island after Crete, though it seems more like a part of the mainland detached from Attica.

123 bottom The landscapes of Skiros, and the rest of the northern Sporades, have a distinctly verdant look compared with the sun-parched scenarios of the islands further south.

Northeast from the Saronic Gulf is Euboea, an island in little more than name due to the two bridges that connect it to the mainland (the charming old bridge, which is approximately 40 meters long, and an ultramodern cable-stayed bridge). In effect, it can be considered continental because of its environmental features, varied landscapes and small factories, which are not found on the other islands. We have to continue further north, as far as the waters off the Pilion peninsula, to find unspoiled scenery in blissful surroundings. Skiros, the most important of the Sporades group, is still partly covered by forests. The town is perched on a steep hill surrounded by dark-green vegetation; until a few years ago it was a center of fine-quality craftmanship, highly regarded for its woodcarving and embroidery; particularly prized were the gold-threaded *zevriedes skirioti*, broad bands worn around the waist over the national costume. Skiros Town now tends to resemble one big bazaar but the island is still one of the most attractive in Greece. While nearby Skiathos and Skopelos can't be classified as mere barren, sun-baked rocks, they are light-years away from the aromatic maquis.

Trees are plentiful again on Thasos and Samothrace, in the far north. The first of the two islands was once a safe anchorage on the route to the gold mines of Thrace: its ancient harbor, dating to the classical period, is one of the few surviving harbors so well preserved. Samothrace is perhaps best known as the original home of the "Winged Victory," the celebrated statue now exhibited in the Louvre. But first and foremost it was the site of cults centered on mysteries and sacrifice, performed in temples whose remains can still be seen. Mount Fengari, soaring to 1600 meters above the Aegean, offers a splendid panorama of the entire northern coastline. In terms of natural beauty both islands are exceptionally well endowed, although the scars left by forest fires each summer are not always quick to heal. Further east, Lesbos is the first in the long chain of "Asian" islands facing the shores of Turkey. Ruled at different times by Arabs, Turks, Venetians and Genoese, Mitilini, the ancient birthplace of Sappho and capital of the famous island, has an inexplicably large harbor for its needs. Until the diaspora of the Greeks of Asia Minor, it was a prominent center of trade and with the handsome neo-classical homes built by its merchants, Mitilini was a far from unattractive place. Miraculously still intact in the northern part of Lesbos is medieval Molivos. Sigri, near the western tip of the island,

boasts a geological rarity: a petrified forest of plane and oak trees, created by an erupting volcano.

Continuing south, we come to Hios, capital of the *mastika* trade (this resin, scraped from mastic bushes – *pistacia terebinthus* and *pistacia lentisca* – was used to make liqueurs and sweets). Hios still offers abundant evidence of its Byzantine and medieval past partly due to the fact that in the 19th century, during the war of independence, the island was abandoned by its inhabitants, fearing continuous attacks launched from the nearby shores of Turkey. Only the monastery of Nea Moni, one of the most important Byzantine monuments on the Greek islands, was never abandoned, its monks obstinately braving the wrath of the Ottoman empire.

Samos, which is renowned world wide for its vase production, acquired a very special meaning for the Turks: after a bloody Samiote uprising against the Ottomans, its name became a synonym for "going to die." Which is one of the reasons why Samos alone among the Greek islands under the dominion of the Sublime Porte, was actually ruled by a Christian governor. The island preserves important testimonies to its former splendor: the Temple of Hera and the ancient capital of the classical period, not far from the present-day village of Pithagorio. A further attraction is the renowned Efpalinion tunnel, in which chapels of Byzantine origin can still be seen.

Patmos – the island of the Apocalpyse – lies about 100 kilometers from Samos. It is an extremely beautiful place, its prevailingly red and yellow landscape dominated by the fortified Monastery of Saint John the Evangelist. It was on this hilltop, overlooking one of the loveliest landscapes in the entire Aegean, that he revealed his vision of the end of the world.

126 top This is the lovely port of Rhodes overlooked by the Fort of St. Nicholas in the background. Hidden below the water are the historically authenticated remains of what used to be one of the Seven Wonders of the World, the Colossus that guarded the entrance to the harbor and was used as a lighthouse for sailors.

126-127 Above the port of Mandraki stands the imposing palace of the Grand Masters of the Knights of Rhodes. The citadel is still intact, a true jewel of Crusader architecture on the road to the Holy Sepulchre.

127 top The court of the palace of the Grand Masters was destroyed by the explosion of a powder-magazine in 1856. The new palace built during the Fascist era should have been used as a residence for Benito Mussolini.

127 center Although the palace of the Grand Masters of Rhodes is only a faithful 20th-century reconstruction from the time of the Italian domination, the fortress has managed to preserve some of its charm: it commemorates on of the fight for the Holy Sepulchre.

THE DODECANESE

Stretching south from Patmos (also part of this archipelago) are the Dodecanese, a region with a very distinctive historical legacy. For centuries life on these islands was directly influenced by the Rhodes-based monastic order of the Knights of St. John, heirs to a considerable part of the treasures and power of the Knights Templar; a major role in their modern history was instead played by the Italians, who governed Rhodes between 1912 and 1948. In many respects the island of Rhodes, capital of the Dodecanese, is the least Greek of the Aegean islands: the fortified citadel built here for their defence by Italian and French monks is not dissimilar to walled cities of Western Europe. Were it not for the bougainvillea and jasmine, the new town might pass for a district of Stockholm, in view of the numerous signs written in Swedish offering Scandinavian-style breakfast. The 15th-century medieval city is a unique testimony to the intermingled cultures of Crusaders and eastern conquerors. Along the Street of the Knights or Odhos Sokratous, mosques stand next door to crenellated buildings, antiques stores to Byzantine churches.

127 bottom Gothic architecture dominates Knights Street, the most austere of the medieval thoroughfares in Rhodes. Here there are the knights "hostels" which are divided by nationality: French, Italian, Spanish, Provençal.

128 top left
Fishermen – the picture shows one from Samo – are still common in the Greek islands. Most of them work for themselves using a family boat rather than for a large fleet.

Lindos, on the east coast of Rhodes, is instead a conventionally Greek town, built beneath an acropolis dated to the 5th century BC. Completing the island's archaeological panorama are the ruins of Ialyssos and Kameiros, the latter sufficiently well preserved to be considered the "Greek Pompei." Each year in spring Petaloudhes, the "Valley of the Butterflies," offers an amazing sight when it fills with thousands and thousands of these colorful creatures. The other islands of the Dodecanese have little in common with Rhodes. Situated close at hand, Simi is dry and barren, but its prosperity as a center of trade in the late 1800s led to the construction around its harbor of handsome neoclassical dwellings, painted in assorted colors and frescoed internally by local artists. Considerably further north but a whole world away from verdant and fertile Rhodes are volcanic Nissiros, known for sulphure mining, Kalimnos, the main sponge-diving port of Greece, and – most distant and easterly of the Greek islands – the microscopic Kastellorizo, put on the map by the Oscar-winning Italian film *Mediterraneo*.

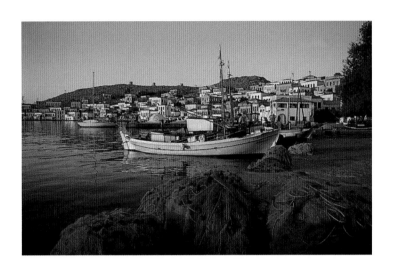

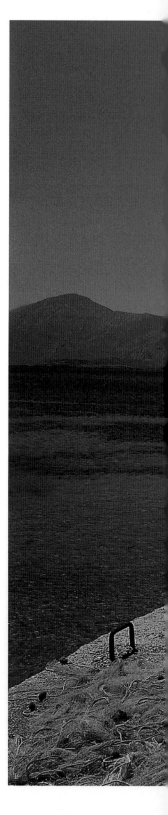

130 top The massive castle at the top of the hill looks over the island of Leros. The new town has been built a short distance from the old building allowing the latter to be better appreciated.

130 center A small cement bridge connects the church of St. Isidore on Leros to the mainland. The fish-filled waters of the bays of the island are as calm as a lagoon.

130 bottom Vathis on the island of Kalimnos is a real fjord. It is one of the "good ports" that the name Kalimnos refers to. The island is one of the most pleasant in the Dodecanese archipelago.

130-131 A small but lively island in the Dodecanese, Leros offers a simple and rustic welcome based on its beautiful beaches and sea where sponge fishing is still an occupation.

131 top The tower shape of the upper part of the house is a typical feature of traditional architecture on Leros. The tower allows the air to cool and the offset apertures encourage ventilation.

INDEX

*136 The Greek flag
flies from every
national monument
and institutional
building. Irrespective
of their political
leanings the Greeks
have strong patriotic
feelings.*

ILLUSTRATION CREDITS

Antonio Attini / Archivio White Star: pages 8, 9 top, 17 top, 72 top left, 84 top right, 96 top left, 104, 105, 110, 111 left, 112 top, 121 center, 125 bottom, 129 center and bottom.
Marcello Bertinetti / Archivio White Star: pages 14 top and bottom, 58 bottom, 60 bottom, 60-61, 80, 81 top, 120-121, 121 bottom, 128 top, 129 top, 136.
Giulio Veggi / Archivio White Star: pages 61 top, 62 top, 63.
Velissarios Voutsas / On Location: pages 13 top, 76, 78-79, 80-81, 83 top, 122 top, 126-127 center and bottom, 70, 70-71, 86, 87, 91, 97 center and bottom.
Ag. Double's: pages 24 right, 25 right, 27 top right, 35 top, 38 left bottom, 40, 41 bottom, 42, 42-43, 60 top, 64 right, 65, 66.
Ag. Luisa Ricciarini: pages 25 left, 31 left bottom, 36, 38 top right, 64 left.
Upi-Corbis: page 48 top.
Archivio Scala: pages 29 bottom, 30 top left, 30-31, 31 right bottom, 69 top.
AKG Photo: pages 24 left, 26 bottom, 40-41, 43, 47 top, 49 bottom, 50, 50-51, 51 top, 52, 53 top, 55 top and center.
Stefano Amantini / Atlantide: pages 92-93, 94-95.
Giulio Andreini: pages 74 top, 79 top, 112 center, 123 center, 125 top.
Stefano Ardito: page 77.
Alberto Biscaro / SIE: page 106 bottom.
Massimo Borchi / Atlantide: pages 11 top, 102 top.
Hervé Champollion / Ag. Top: page 74-75.
V. Constatineas / On Location: page 58 center, 90 top right.
Anne Conway: pages 10-11, 78 top, 83 bottom.
Guido Cozzi / Atlantide: page 112 bottom.
Giovanni Dagli Orti: pages 66-67, 68, 111 right bottom.
Tim de Waele / Corbis / Contrasto: pages 14-15, 15.
George Diamantopoulos: page 12 top.
Joël Ducange / Ag. Top: pages 58-59, 59 top left.
Nevio Doz / Ag. Marka: page 123 top.
E.T. Archive: pages 28 bottom, 29 top, 34 bottom.
Farabolafoto: pages 47 bottom, 53 bottom, 54-55.
Gigliola Foschi / Focus Team: page 72-73.
Fototeca Storica Nazionale: pages 46 bottom, 47 center, 49 top, 51 bottom.
Gräfenhaim / Bildagentur Huber / Sime: pages 82 top, 82-83.
Loukas Hapsis / On Location: pages 10 bottom, 12-13, 85, 99 top left, 102 top, 103, 121 top, 124 top.
Peter Hollenbach / Das Photoarchiv: page 97 top.
Index, Firenze: pages 32 left, 44 top, 45 right, 46-47, 48-49.
Johanna Huber / SIME: pages 8-9, 16-17, 62-63, 106-107, 107 top, 108-109, 111 top right and center, 112-113, 113 center, 114 bottom, 115/118, 119, 124-125, 130, 130-131, 131.
Vassilis Kostakos: page 94 top.
Marco Leopardi / SIE: page 17 bottom.
W. Louvet / Ag. Visa: pages 90 top left, 94 center.
Mary Evans Picture Library: pages 2/7, 32-33, 33 bottom, 34-35, 39.
Marco Melodia / Realy Easy Star: page 122-123.
M. Mastrolillo / SIE: pages 58 top, 79 bottom, 84 top left.
Clairy Mostafellou / On Location: page 72 top right.
Photobank: pages 3-6, 14 center.
Photo Nimatallah / Ag. Luisa Ricciarini: pages 26 top, 69 bottom.
Andrea Pistolesi: pages 1, 10 top, 20-21, 106 top, 107 top, 113 top and bottom, 114 top, 120 top.
Massimo Pizzocaro / On Location: pages 63 top, 102 bottom.
Marco Polo - F. Bouillot: page 94 bottom.
Ripani / SIME: pages 99 top right, 102-103.
Giovanni Simeone / SIME: pages 13 bottom, 17 center, 22-23, 84-85 86-87, 88, 88-89, 90-91, 96 top right, 96-97, 98, 98-99, 102-103, 103 top.
The Ancient Art Architecture Collection: page 27 bottom.
The British Museum: pages 28 top, 30 bottom, 35 bottom.
Sandro Vannini / Ag. Franca Speranza: pages 59 top right, 75.
Werner Forman Archive / Index, Firenze: page 41 top.

Map by Elisabetta Ferrero